BARRIERS TO LEARNING

The Case for Integrated Mental Health Services in Schools

DEBRA S. LEAN and VINCENT A. COLUCCI

ROWMAN & LITTLEFIELD EDUCATION
A division of
ROWMAN & LITTLEFIELD PUBLISHERS, INC.
Lanham • New York • Toronto • Plymouth, UK

Published by Rowman & Littlefield Education
A division of Rowman & Littlefield Publishers, Inc.
A wholly owned subsidiary of The Rowman & Littlefield Publishing Group, Inc.
4501 Forbes Boulevard, Suite 200, Lanham, Maryland 20706
www.rowmaneducation.com

Estover Road, Plymouth PL6 7PY, United Kingdom

British Library Cataloguing in Publication Information Available

Library of Congress Cataloging-in-Publication Data
Lean, Debra S.
  Barriers to learning : the case for integrated mental health services in schools / Debra S. Lean and Vincent A. Colucci.
       p. cm.
  Includes bibliographical references.
  ISBN 978-1-60709-637-5 (cloth : alk. paper) — ISBN 978-1-60709-638-2 (pbk. : alk. paper) — ISBN 978-1-60709-639-9 (electronic)
  1. School children—Mental health. 2. School children—Mental health services. 3. Students—Mental health services. 4. Schools—Sociological aspects. 5. Crisis intervention (Mental health services) 6. School health services. I. Colucci, Vincent A. II. Title.
  LB3430.L43 2010
  371.7'13—dc22   2010005284

⊗™ The paper used in this publication meets the minimum requirements of American National Standard for Information Sciences—Permanence of Paper for Printed Library Materials, ANSI/NISO Z39.48-1992.

Printed in the United States of America

CONTENTS

LIST OF FIGURES

FOREWORD

There has been a longstanding debate on the relative roles of non-school and school factors in influencing student achievement. In rough terms the conclusion has been that both sets of forces are critical. In my reading they account for about half the variance, each in the impact it has on the life chances of children. The obvious answer is that we should seek solutions that combine, indeed integrate key non-school and school factors.

This is where Debra Lean's and Vincent Colucci's *Barriers to Learning* comes into play. There are very few, if any books in the literature that furnish a grounded account of the major historical and current barriers to integrating mental health services and school life that also make the practical case for such integration. *Barriers to Learning* makes a critical, powerful, and timely contribution to making schools and school systems effective for all children. Well-written, clear, and compelling, this is a must-read book for education reformers.

The prologue on a hypothetical, but all-too-real ABC school district grabs us from page one, immersing the reader into the frustrating realization that the current nonintegrated system does not and cannot work for kids or for their teachers and administrators. You can almost experience with the teachers and administrators the inevitable downhill discouragement that well-intended educators experience as they try to cope with the piecemeal and fragmented bits with which they have to work.

Subsequent chapters carefully document the barriers to learning that are built into the present system. "Biological-psychological barriers" are chronicled. Learning disabilities, attention deficit disorders, and related anxieties take their toll on both slow learners and gifted students. Similar treatment is given to "environmental and circumstantial barriers" in the home and related non-school life of children that, again, take their toll on the school's capacity to cope.

Then frustratingly we see how current "intervention strategies" are woefully inadequate ranging from absence of treatment to ineffective and too-little-too-late responses to obvious learning needs of children.

Then in a breakthrough chapter, Lean and Colucci describe how the education system and the mental health system are two badly leaking ships that pass each other in the night. With 15 to 20 percent of children having serious mental or emotional problems (and obviously higher percentages in disadvantages areas) it becomes obvious that two handicapped silos only exacerbate the problem.

The careful foundation work in the book that identifies and describes the barriers, and especially the analyses that show a complete absence of a *system*, enables the authors to link the problems with a directional solution. Their proposed School-based Integrated Support Services Model (SISSM) is sound in its own right, but all the more convincing because the reader has been treated to a careful documentation of the myriad problems that vulnerable students face in the current system. Lean and Colucci present a convincing case for fully integrated evidence-based treatment that intervenes early and as often as required to serve the entire population. In addition to the model itself the authors also identify the crucial role of leadership that will be required to develop and implement the SISSM in practice.

Finally, Lean and Colucci return to the new and improved ABC hypothetical district now using SISSM and describe the life of the school as it operates within the new system. We see the lives of children and teachers become dramatically different in a system that now integrates mental health services and schooling in concert.

The proposals in *Barriers to Learn* are consistent with my own recent ideas for accomplishing "whole system reform" in an effort to make *All Systems Go* (Fullan 2010). Lean and Colucci have gone a step further by integrating non-school and non-academic factors that are essential to full system reform. This is a book of "barriers and solutions" convincingly argued and presented.

Michael Fullan

professor emeritus

Ontario Institute for Studies in Education, University of Toronto

REFERENCE

Fullan, M. (2010). *All Systems Go*. Thousand Oaks, CA: Corwin Press; and Toronto, Ontario Principals Council.

ACKNOWLEDGMENTS

I thank my coauthor, colleague, and friend, Vincent Colucci, for the opportunity to be part of this project. His wisdom, foresight, and aptitude with the written word guided the journey, from our early discussions about education and mental health, through numerous manuscript revisions and on to the finished product.

I thank my husband, Martin, for his love, patience, and support always and especially throughout this endeavor, for giving me excellent feedback when I attempted to explain the numerous versions of the model, for his valuable insights into government systems, and for "holding the fort" while I was researching and writing. I thank my children, Paul and Jay, for being the wonderful young people they are and for their understanding and support during this work. I thank my sister, Shelley, and her family for their support. I thank my colleagues and friends, both within and outside Dufferin-Peel for their support.

I thank Laura Rood and Lori Attinello for their ability to quickly and expertly turn our scribbles on paper into elegant graphics. I thank many friends and colleagues, both within and outside of Dufferin-Peel, who commented on various versions of the model and gave me valued advice.

Lastly, I thank my parents, Stan and Lilyan Lean, for instilling in me a love for learning and a passion for helping children and youth. It is to their memory that I dedicate this book.

Debra Susan Lean
December 3, 2009

Ideas remain ideas until they are brought to fruition. In our attempt to accomplish this goal, I could not have hoped for a more knowledgeable and skilful coauthor and colleague than my friend, Debra Lean. Her tenacity for research and unwavering commitment to professionalism helped us stay the course.

I thank my wife, Leslie, for her ongoing support and for her wisdom as an experienced educator. I thank my son, Lee, and my daughter, Emma, for their keen interest and encouragement. I thank my sister Connie for all her support.

I thank my friends and colleagues, both within and outside of Dufferin-Peel, for their personal and professional contributions. I thank Lori Attinello and Laura Rood for the magic they brought to the graphics of this book.

Lastly, I thank my parents, Luigi and Lucia Colucci, for championing the value and richness of lifelong learning, and for showing us the true meaning of altruism. It is to the memory of my father, Luigi, that I dedicate this book.

Vincent Anthony Colucci
December 3, 2009

INTRODUCTION

*B*arriers to Learning: The Case for Integrated Mental Health Services in Schools has emerged from our school-based perspective and over fifty years of experience in both education support and mental health intervention services.

Recent trends in education reform have concentrated on improving student achievement. Closing the achievement gap is a primary objective. Generally, improvements in leadership and pedagogy along with increased accountability are seen as the solutions. Current developments in child and youth mental health reform recommend providing specific mental health services in schools. This change is recommended as a significant part of an overall plan to address the increasing prevalence of mental health problems in children and youth.

Educators are acknowledging the relationship between achievement and student mental health. Partnerships with mental health agencies are rapidly being developed to address these problems in students.

This book presents the case for integrating the mental health and education sectors to address barriers to learning. In our opinion, it is essential to guide and manage the mental health partnerships that are coming into schools to avoid the situation where these services are simply "co-located" in the schools. We have developed a model of service delivery that integrates mental health services for students through careful collaboration with community organizations. The model emphasizes the core role of student support services professionals in schools.

The book begins with a narrative prologue that looks inside fictitious elementary and secondary classrooms. Examples of barriers to learning are presented through specific students in the classrooms. Also illustrated are current methods of addressing these barriers, both from school-based as well as community-based services.

Chapter 1 introduces school-based and school-linked services and the professionals who deliver them. Barriers to learning are defined and various classifications are discussed, specifically biological-psychological and environmental-circumstantial. A graphic representation of barriers to learning and outcomes of intervention is presented.

Chapter 2 discusses the increasing prevalence of biological-psychological barriers to learning and how they affect student functioning in the classroom. These barriers to learning are presented in an order of what we believe to be the frequency of referrals for intervention at school.

Chapter 3 begins with a discussion of several environmental-circumstantial barriers as well as their prevalence and effect on student functioning. Next, we discuss the problems inherent in labeling students with individual pathologies when their difficulties are related to their particular environment and circumstances.

Chapter 4 presents the consequences of inadequate or nonintervention of the barriers to learning presented in chapters 2 and 3. We introduce the hypothetical Multi-Ripple Effect for students who are not facing barriers to learning. These students may be affected by their classmates who have not received adequate and timely intervention for their barriers to learning.

Chapter 5 presents current literature on barriers to learning from both the education and child and youth mental health fields. We begin examining recent initiatives in education reform that are addressing barriers to learning. We discuss current special and alternative education practices and theorize that these practices may not adequately meet the needs of all students facing barriers to learning.

Research and initiatives in child and youth mental health reform are presented. This is followed by a discussion of school-based mental health as a new area of research and practice that has responded to calls for administering certain child and youth mental health interventions on school premises.

Chapter 6 presents different school system approaches to address barriers to learning. We introduce and discuss the advantages of population-based services for both academic- and behavior-based barriers to learning.

Chapter 7 introduces a model of support services delivery to schools that addresses barriers to learning through education and child and youth mental health sector collaboration. The School-based Integrated Support

Services Model (SISSM) is presented on both a large- and small-scale basis, along with details for evaluation.

The book concludes with an epilogue that revisits the fictional teachers and students introduced in the prologue. Here, the classes are part of the SISSM system. The differences in the efficiency and effectiveness of interventions for addressing barriers to learning are highlighted.

PROLOGUE

ABC District School Board

A BC District School Board is a fictional publicly funded school board in a large, diverse urban area. The board has utilized a number of evidence-based initiatives to increase student achievement. These initiatives include the following:

- Support for developing professional learning communities for educators as a means of knowledge exchange and professional development
- Training and support in following up student assessment results through data-based decision making
- Training and support for differentiated instruction and high yield strategies
- Support for parent involvement, particularly through parent councils/parent teacher associations
- Increased accountability through government-mandated large-scale assessments in reading, writing, and mathematics

ABC District School Board also employs school-based student support services professionals, including psychologists, social workers, child and youth counselors and allied health professionals such as speech-language pathologists and physical and occupational therapists.[1] Although these services are part of the publicly funded system, and are considered to be a significant and integral part of education, they are not mandated. Consequently, the decision as to which disciplines and how many are hired rests primarily with each school district and its ability to fund such services.

Due to the small number of student support service professionals employed by this particular board, their work tends to be limited to assisting individual students with severe problems and the most pressing needs, and determining individual students' eligibility for special education services.

EFG ELEMENTARY SCHOOL: MS. W.'S GRADE 3 CLASS

EFG Elementary is a school in ABC School District with a student population of 632. It is 9:08 a.m. on a Monday morning. The announcements are over. The class of twenty-five students takes several minutes to settle. The teacher, Ms. W., begins her lesson by asking the class to take out their notebooks, pencils, and textbooks.

The first half of the morning progresses relatively smoothly, as Ms. W. begins to implement some of the new techniques she learned recently at an in-service for differentiated instruction. She knows all her students' scores on the recent gradewide reading assessment; they are clearly displayed on the data wall in the primary level resource room.

It is February and a number of students who scored the lowest in the recent reading assessment have made limited progress. Ms. W. and the literacy specialist teacher who visits the school weekly continue with their efforts at helping these students. Ms. W. suspects that at least two of these students have undiagnosed learning disabilities.

The students with reading problems will at some point have a psychological assessment; however, in Ms. W.'s school district, it may be some time before the assessment takes place. Meanwhile, she has consulted her administrator and the special education resource teacher on how to further improve these students' reading.

These students with the low reading scores are not the only ones having difficulty in the classroom.

- Cameron is prepared and ready to work, but is having difficulty focusing because of several distractions happening around him.
  - Beth sits at Cameron's table grouping. She often does not remember what she has to do and calls out to Ms. W. for help.
  - Carl shoves Jamie, a student not facing barriers to learning, who sits next to Cameron, and Jamie falls off his chair. Jamie decides

that he has had enough and retaliates by getting up and hitting Carl back.

- ○ While Ms. W. is busy addressing the disruption Carl and Jamie created, Cameron is becoming increasingly frustrated and forgets what he needs to work on.

Ms. W. brings order back to the class. More disruptions occur.

- Billy, a student who is a slower learner, has yet to begin his work. He is making noises and moving his desk and chair around. Ms. W. chooses to ignore Billy's behavior, but Cameron is unable to do so.
- Ms. W. looks around and is happy to see Kyle in class today. Kyle, who is new to the school this year, is frequently absent. He has missed thirty-five days of school to date. He does not know what to do on the assignment, so Ms. W. briefly goes over the lesson that he missed during his latest absence.
- Cameron now has his hand raised and a question to ask. Knowing that Cameron is a strong student, Ms. W. feels he can wait or solve the problem himself. She asks him to wait and continues to work with Kyle.

STUDENT'S BACKGROUND INFORMATION AND SUPPORT SERVICES TEAM INVOLVEMENT

- Beth was seen by the school psychologist earlier this year and was diagnosed with a severe learning disability. She was on the assessment waiting list for a considerable amount of time, which exacerbated her anxiety about her learning difficulties. She has yet to develop independent work skills and continues to be a very anxious student who is on a community-based agency waiting list for counseling.
- Ms. W. knows that Carl has a diagnosis of attention deficit hyperactivity disorder and oppositional defiant disorder. He was diagnosed four years ago by his family doctor when his mother expressed her concerns with his lack of compliance and difficulties managing his behavior.
  - ○ Carl was prescribed medication but Ms. W. suspects that it is not consistently administered at home.
  - ○ Ms. W. recently became aware that Carl, his brother, and mother left the family home and are currently living in a shelter. The

school principal informed her of these recent developments when he received a copy of the restraining order against Carl's father. Subsequently, the principal called the social worker to become directly involved with Carl and his family as well as liaise with the community-based agencies servicing the family.

- o As a result of all these developments, Carl will likely be the first student to be discussed at the school's support services team meeting next month.
- Billy recently had a psychological assessment.
  - o Billy was found to be functioning in the below average range of intelligence.
  - o A previous speech-language pathology assessment determined that his language skills are mildly to moderately delayed.
  - o Billy has an individual education plan developed by Ms. W., the school's special education resource teacher, psychologist, and speech-language pathologist.
  - o Billy has low self-esteem, and at times compensates with aggressive, defiant, and disruptive behavior.
  - o The team referred Billy to a social skills group run by the school child and youth counselor. During one of the sessions, Billy got frustrated and threw a chair, injuring the child and youth counselor. As a result, he was suspended. His parents are appealing the suspension on mitigating circumstances, particularly Billy's learning difficulties.
- Kyle has been referred to the school social worker for attendance issues.
  - o Ms. W. knows, from discussions with the school social worker, that he stays home watching over his mother during her frequent bouts of depression.
  - o Kyle's mother has refused to participate in counseling; consequently the school social worker is limited primarily to addressing the attendance issue.
  - o Kyle also has difficulty reading. Ms. W. has been unable to determine the cause or extent of his reading difficulty due to his frequent absences.

After morning recess, Ms. W. begins the math program. Robin returns to class with Mrs. S., his educational resource worker. Robin is a child with a rare chromosomal disorder. Children with this disorder have a severe intellectual disability, poor muscle tone, small stature, and challenging behaviors. Robin's receptive language skills, although low, are better than his minimal expressive language skills.

Robin is currently being taught to use an augmentative communication system where he can point to pictures on a device and the words are spoken aloud. Robin also has a high activity level and can seldom stay seated and attend for more than one minute. He spent most of his grade 2 year in the hospital dealing with heart surgery and ensuing complications.

Robin is becoming increasingly aggressive and Mrs. S. had removed him from class to a small room to calm him down. Although Robin appears to be calmed down when he returns to the classroom, he runs to the door when Mrs. S. starts his individualized math program. The rest of the class, as instructed, tries to ignore the interruption and Mrs. S. again calms Robin and redirects his behavior.

Ms. W. notices that Kyle, as well as two other students, is not participating in the lively discussions taking place at each table. Cameron and Jamie are not fully engaged in their work and they each call out for help. She understands why Jamie is having difficulty today, but as she redirects Cameron's attention back to the mathematics work, she wonders if there is anything in particular bothering him today.

In spite of the "turbulence" in her class this morning, Ms. W. manages to cover the literacy and numeracy curriculum. However, the afternoon brings a different set of challenges. Beth becomes upset because she cannot keep up with the work. Carl gets sent, yet again, and Jamie, for the first time ever, to the principal's office. Carl spends the rest of the afternoon in the office and Jamie gets sent back to class. When Jamie arrives, he is visibly angry, sits at his desk, and finds it very difficult to focus on his work. Beth continues to need Ms. W.'s attention.

Kyle approaches Ms. W., complaining of a stomachache. He looks pale and stressed. He tells Ms. W. that he feels sick and needs to go home. Mrs. W. sends him to the office where his aunt picks him up. Cameron puts his hand up to ask a question.

XYZ SECONDARY SCHOOL: MR. M.'S GRADE 10 ENGLISH CLASS

XYZ Secondary School is a midsized secondary school in ABC School District. Mr. M. is an English teacher. He teaches three classes in a two semester system: one grade 12 university stream class, one grade 10 junior college stream class, and a grade 11 class for students going into the world of work.

We join Mr. M. in his grade 10 junior college stream classroom. He has just given the students an assignment and is trying to mark term papers while they work.

Many students are doing well in the course, and are able to work independently on the current assignment. He is pleased to see that two students with learning disabilities are taking advantage of the special software package the school has provided to them that includes text to speech as well as speech to text programs. He has noticed that their writing skills have improved considerably.

Mr. M. reads George's paper and sees that he has done quite well on the assignment. He knows that George has benefited from the credit recovery program for mathematics provided by a specialized teacher who helps struggling students. As a result, George is much more motivated to learn, his achievement in his other courses has increased, and he is generally less disruptive in class.

Mr. M. is pleased to see the academic support initiatives working for some of his students; however, he is very concerned about some others.

- Rena's paper alarms Mr. M. He is aware that she has a diagnosis of depression and is on medication prescribed by her family doctor. She has written a story about suicide, again. Mr. M. was present at the school's last support services team meeting where her need for more intensive treatment at a community agency was discussed. The school psychologist will be counseling Rena until community treatment commences.
- Jessica's paper is longer than Mr. M. requested. It is off topic and rambling. Earlier in the year, Jessica produced A-level work; however, Mr. M. has seen her work deteriorate over the past few months. He is aware that Jessica was diagnosed in grade 8 with an anxiety disorder and was treated with counseling and medication by the Child and Adolescent Mental Health team at the local hospital. This treatment was helpful and she was discharged. However, she is still experiencing difficulties at school, particularly test and exam anxiety.
- The next paper is from Evan. Evan is a student who has a long history of learning and behavioral problems. Evan was diagnosed with a learning disability in grade 3. His parents never accepted the diagnosis and continue to blame the school for all of Evan's problems.

Although Evan and his family have been referred many times for counseling at a community agency, his parents refused to attend and the agency eventually closed the case.

- ○ Aside from Evan's learning difficulties, his sporadic attendance has contributed to his poor academic and social development. Today Evan is in class, and he is being disruptive. He is bothering two neighboring students who generally do well. Lately, they seem to be attracted by Evan's antics and Mr. M. is concerned that they may compromise their own academic progress as a result.

- ○ Mr. M. also referred Evan to the credit recovery program. Evan has met once with the teacher. Evan was given the option to transfer to the district's School to Work Program. He refused. The specialist teacher discussed Evan's potential course failure with the guidance counselor and the vice principal.

- There is no paper from Jayden. Jayden is a bright student but has great difficulty with written language. Although capable, he produces minimal work in class. He is also impulsive and distracts others. He is failing most of his subjects, and his teachers suspect that he may have an attention disorder. At the last support services team meeting, additional classroom strategies were discussed that would help Jayden while he waits for a psychological assessment.

- Bryan has not handed in his paper. Bryan works evenings at the local supermarket. Bryan's father is on disability and his mother works at a donut shop. Bryan often sleeps in and misses his first class, which is English. He was not in class today. Bryan normally does well academically, but lately, his preoccupation with family issues is affecting his marks.

- Ray's paper, like much of his other work, is below his potential.
  - ○ Known to the school as a student who frequently abuses substances, Ray has had several suspensions and risks expulsion. He has also had police involvement.
  - ○ As he often does, Ray arrives late and disrupts the class. When Ray was absent last week, the class was more settled, the students were more attentive, and Mr. M. was able to get through the lesson without interruptions. Mr. M. has been unsuccessful at contacting Ray's parents, as has the school social worker.

- Patrick's paper is a good paper for his ability level. Mr. M. is concerned about how Ray, Jayden, and Evan are having a negative influence on Patrick. Patrick, who normally has excellent attention skills, is increasingly having difficulty concentrating.

- Chase's paper is well done, but Mr. M. has concerns about his well-being. He suspects that Chase is being bullied by the other boys, but when he asks, Chase refuses to discuss the situation. He is also concerned with Chase's increasing absenteeism and the potential for academic difficulties.
- Jaclyn is an A student who is concerned about maintaining her good grades. Her paper reflects this concern.

Both Mr. M. and Ms. W. are similar in their approach to their students. They are caring, dedicated teachers who have seen improvements in many students. However, they are both concerned about a number of their students who are not responding to evidence-based high-quality academic strategies. The students they are most concerned with are those who fit into a troubling statistic, the 20 percent of students who have significant mental health concerns and the 80 percent of those particular students whose mental health needs are not properly being met.

Ms. W. and Mr. M. feel that in the past there did not seem to be that many students in classrooms with severe emotional and behavior problems. The teachers are also concerned with many students not facing barriers to learning who may be affected by the increasing number of students with a variety of needs that are not adequately addressed.

1

BARRIERS TO LEARNING

The fictitious classes in the preceding prologue provide a profile of a present-day classroom in a publicly funded education system. The purpose is to gain familiarity with common barriers to learning and how these barriers challenge learning and teaching. Researchers have identified that currently, there are more students in classrooms with varied and complex mental health issues than in the past.[1]

Studies have been consistent in indicating that approximately 15 to 20 percent of children and youth have diagnosable mental health disorders, and about 75 percent of this group of children and youth do not receive treatment or receive substandard treatment.[2,3] This statistic translates to four to six students in every classroom with a potentially diagnosable mental health disorder.

It is our opinion that the increase in mental health issues in children and youth, as well as the move toward inclusion, has changed the dynamics of the typical elementary and secondary classroom. We illustrated this dynamic in the prologue. The students in the prologue exhibited varying degrees of academic underachievement and behaviors that were directly related to the barriers to learning that they faced. There were also students not facing barriers to learning in each class who were affected by some of their classmates' behaviors.

It is important to gain a clear understanding of the breadth (types), depth (prevalence), and effects on achievement of barriers to learning that exist in publicly funded classrooms today. This understanding is required in order to make the case for student support services involvement to lessen the effects of barriers to learning, thereby freeing the students to learn and the teachers to teach.

Student support services professionals normally include psychologists, social workers, child and youth counselors, and allied health professionals including speech-language pathologists, occupational therapists, and physical therapists.

There are different manifestations of student support services professionals in schools. They can be classified as either school-based or school-linked. School-based services are

- Often employed by school systems
- Based in schools (provide services at school sites for the school year)
- Are an integral part of the educational system
- Are supervised by same-discipline professionals based in the school system
- Assigned to their placements according to the needs of the school system
- Accountable to the school system that is responsible for the governance of services

School-linked services are

- Employed by community organizations/agencies
- Generally based in the community (but can provide services at school sites)
- Not normally an integral part of the education system
- Supervised by professionals based in the community organization/ agency
- Assigned to school placements according to the needs of the community organization/agency
- Often temporary/short-term/project-based
- Accountable to the community organization/agency that is responsible for the governance of services

DEFINITION OF BARRIERS TO LEARNING

- A factor, condition, or situation that obstructs or impedes academic progress
- Can be temporary (short-term, long-term) or permanent
- Effect of barriers to learning range from mild (e.g., lower marks) to severe (e.g., dropping out)

CLASSIFICATION OF BARRIERS TO LEARNING

• Academic (learning disorders)
• Nonacademic (emotional/behavioral disorders; mental health difficulties)

This book proposes a more in-depth classification of barriers to learning than the academic/nonacademic dichotomy. Broadening the classification leads to a more complete understanding of barriers to learning and the consequences for both the students who experience them as well as their classmates. This broader classification is crucial in determining and implementing appropriate and timely interventions to address these barriers.

Our conceptualization of barriers to learning includes two types, as well as negative and positive outcomes based on the nature of intervention.

• Biological-psychological barriers to learning
  ○ Constitutional/innate predisposition in individual students
    • Examples include learning disorders such as developmental disorders or learning disabilities
  ○ Psychological/emotional disorders
    • Examples include anxiety and conduct disorders
• Environmental-circumstantial barriers to learning
  ○ Based on student's environment, context, and circumstances
    • Examples include change in parental caregivers and economic status
• Nature of interventions and resulting outcomes
  ○ Positive outcomes when barriers to learning are effectively addressed
    • Examples include amelioration of symptoms, chronic care
  ○ Negative outcomes when barriers to learning are not addressed adequately or not dealt with at all
    • Examples include bullying, absenteeism, family dysfunction

This conceptualization of barriers to learning and outcomes of intervention is represented in figure 1.1. The middle panel represents both types of barriers as well as when they intersect. The panel immediately to the right represents timely and adequate intervention. The next panel to the right represents positive outcomes. Barrier reduction and prevention provides amelioration of symptoms or adjustment, while judicious management provides chronic care for barriers that cannot be reduced.

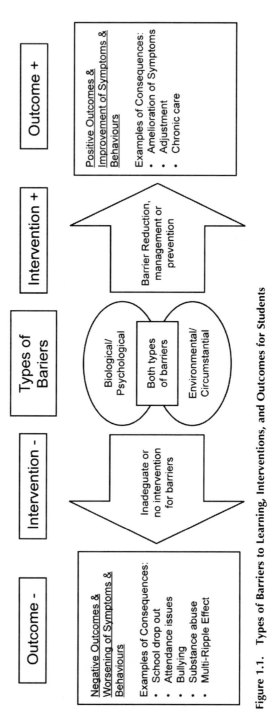

Figure 1.1. Types of Barriers to Learning, Interventions, and Outcomes for Students

Inadequate or nonintervention of barriers to learning is represented to the immediate left of the center panel. The next panel to the left represents negative outcomes, such as worsening of symptoms and behavior.

As seen in figure 1.1, the division of biological-psychological and environmental-circumstantial barriers to learning is not exclusive; there are some barriers that fit into both sections. It is also important to understand that many disorders occur together, and it is not unusual for children and youth to have more than one disorder, which is often referred to as co-morbidity.

The diagnosis of disorders in children and youth is a complex task and occasionally certain reactions to environmental circumstances can be misinterpreted as symptoms indicative of a biological or psychological problem. Behaviors such as inattentiveness, aggression, fearfulness, and poor adaptability can be considered as normal responses to stressful situations in young children. TRAUMA/PTSD

Therefore, careful differential diagnostic procedures should be performed by qualified professionals who consider symptoms with respect to frequency, duration, and level of functional impairment, all within the context of normal developmental variations.

School-based student support professionals are in a unique position to make accurate determinations of the nature of students' barriers to learning and provide or recommend appropriate interventions. We propose that the nature of this intervention be population-based, that is, universal prevention applied to all students, targeted interventions applied to selected at-risk students, and intensive interventions for students with severe needs.

We believe that efficiently addressing all types of barriers to learning is best accomplished by integrating school-based and school-linked services based on locally determined needs, as presented in the School-based Integrated Support Services Model (SISSM).

2

BIOLOGICAL-PSYCHOLOGICAL
BARRIERS TO LEARNING

B iological-psychological conditions are commonly the first and often the only classification of barriers to learning that is considered when students are experiencing difficulties. We present these barriers not in order of their prevalence rates but rather by how often, in our opinion, they are referred for some type of intervention at school. Each barrier is defined and prevalence rates are presented. The manner in which these barriers manifest in the classroom is described.

Schools often focus primarily on academic performance for their students facing biological-psychological barriers to learning. However, as seen below, some of these students can have co-occurring mental health disorders, including slow learners and those with learning disabilities and speech and language disorders.

BARRIERS TO LEARNING COMMONLY
REFERRED FOR INTERVENTION AT SCHOOL

LEARNING DISABILITIES[1]

Learning disabilities generally occur in individuals with at least average intelligence and can range in severity from mild to severe. These disorders are usually diagnosed when a student produces unexpectedly low academic achievement or achievement that is sustainable only by extremely high levels of effort and support. Learning disabilities are sometimes referred to by the specific academic problem the student has, that is, disorders in reading, mathematics, or written expression. Students can have difficulties in one or more of these academic areas.

Learning disabilities are mainly conceptualized as a variety of disorders that affect lifelong learning. Impairments usually occur in at least one area of information processing, including phonological, language, perceptual-motor, visual-spatial, memory, attention, processing speed, and executive functions (e.g., planning, monitoring, and metacognitive abilities).

These processing difficulties are manifested in the classroom as academic achievement that is significantly lower than expected considering the individual's intellectual functioning. Areas of academic difficulty include oral language (e.g., listening, speaking, understanding), reading (e.g., decoding, comprehension), written language (e.g., spelling, written expression), and mathematics (e.g., computation, problem solving). As well, there can be difficulties in organizational and social skills.

Recent practices in the United States stemming from legislation utilize a response to intervention (RTI) approach to identify students with learning disabilities in the school system. These students are identified when they fail to respond to evidence-based classroom instruction as well as more intense instructional interventions.

Learning disabilities are prevalent in schools and account for the highest percentages of students receiving special education services in Canada and the United States at approximately 45 percent. Drop-out rates for students with learning disabilities has been reported to be approximately 40 percent, which is 1.5 times the average rate.

Learning disabilities are the most common long-term condition affecting children and youth. Prevalence rates range between 2 to 11 percent, depending on the definition and how they are diagnosed.

Regardless of the particular definition utilized, the prevalence of learning disabilities has been rising in past years. Data show that placement in learning disability programs in the United States has tripled to 6 percent of all children enrolled in public schools. Some researchers have hypothesized that this situation may be related to chronic low level exposure to environmental toxins such as lead and air pollution. The increasing prevalence rate of learning disabilities has also been connected with factors such as poverty. However, some of this increase in prevalence can be explained by passage of special education legislation and availability of funds specific to special education.

Psychiatric diagnoses are not uncommon in students with learning disabilities. Many are diagnosed with attention deficit hyperactivity disorder (ADHD). Depression, anxiety, and conduct disorders can also occur with learning disabilities. These dual diagnoses, also known as concurrent or comorbid diagnoses, further complicate and ultimately affect academic functioning. However, early diagnosis and appropriate intervention can often prevent development of additional psychiatric problems.

Students with learning disabilities require specialized and long-term interventions at school, home, and in the community in order to be successful. Interventions need to include remediation of skill deficits, appropriate accommodations, and the development of compensatory strategies, self-advocacy, and sometimes counseling to deal with decreased self-esteem.

Individuals with learning disabilities need to understand the complexity of their diagnosis. It is important that the students, their family, and those who teach them, have a clear understanding of the nature of their particular disorder, as well as their strengths and weaknesses. In fact, Levine has coined the term *demystification* to describe a clearly delineated program to explain strengths and weaknesses to these students that helps them to accept assistance and learn how to advocate for themselves.

Gifted–Learning Disabilities

Giftedness can also occur along with learning disabilities. This situation can be difficult to diagnose. These students often achieve at an average level, which is unknowingly below their true potential. If these students are referred to a school support services team, it is often for behavior and not learning problems. These students may have some awareness of their intelligence and become frustrated and act out when they begin to experience academic difficulties.

Prevalence of gifted–learning disabilities ranges from 2 to 5 percent of the children with learning disabilities. Bright students with behavior difficulties should be referred for a school-based comprehensive psychological assessment. It is also important to be able to offer counseling to these students, as many have spent years in frustration and confusion concerning their unidentified exceptionalities, which may be manifested by feelings of failure, worthlessness, low self-esteem, and anger.

ATTENTION DEFICIT DISORDERS[2]

Attention deficit hyperactivity disorders (ADHD) comprise a trio of impairments:

- inattention (distractibility)
- impulsivity
- hyperactivity

The DSM-IV–TR (*Diagnostic and Statistic Manual of Mental Disorders,* 4th ed. with text revisions) from the American Psychiatric Association (2000) categorizes three subtypes:

1. Attention Deficit/Hyperactivity Disorder, Primarily Hyperactive-Impulsive Type
   - Symptoms: motor restlessness, being fidgety, talking excessively, difficulty remaining seated or playing quietly and impulsive behavior (e.g., blurting out answers before questions are completed, difficulty waiting for turns, frequently interrupting or intruding on others)
2. Attention Deficit/Hyperactivity Disorder, Primarily Inattentive Type
   - Symptoms: difficulty sustaining attention, listening to and following through with instructions, organizing tasks, being distracted by outside or inside stimuli (e.g., thoughts), careless mistakes in schoolwork, inattention (distractibility), and forgetfulness
3. Attention Deficit/Hyperactivity Disorder, Combined Type
   - Describes individuals where both hyperactive-impulsive and inattentive symptom sets occur

These symptoms have to appear before seven years of age and must impair functioning in two or more settings for the child (home, school, and community) and not be accounted for by any other childhood mental health disorder.

Recent research has reconceptualized ADHD as a cognitive problem in working memory and executive function. Direct instruction of cognitive strategies for students with ADHD has been shown to reduce behavior symptoms, specifically inattention. The prevalence rate for ADHD in school-age children, when similar diagnostic procedures are utilized, varies between 2 and 9 percent although some have estimated the prevalence rate to be as high as 16 percent.

The diagnosis of ADHD has generated considerable controversy. It has been portrayed at best as a benign condition and at worst as a myth or fraud. However, there is overwhelming international scientific evidence that ADHD is a neurologically based disorder. Without treatment, this disorder can lead to serious impairment, specifically in the areas of education, family, community, and occupational functioning.

Some of this controversy arises from difficulty diagnosing attention disorders. The characteristic symptoms of ADHD (inattention, impulsivity, and hyperactivity) are characteristic of many other childhood conditions, particularly anxiety, depression, and pervasive developmental disorders. In addition, children with language-based learning disabilities may appear restless and distractible due to difficulty understanding classroom instruction and expectations.

Differential diagnosis determines whether a child or youth has a specific diagnosis or has more than one diagnosis (comorbidity) when there are similar symptoms. Psychological assessment (including school observation and data) can rule out comorbid disorders. These assessments are in fact called for in the practice guidelines for both the Canadian ADHD Research Alliance and the American Academy of Child and Adolescent Psychiatry.

Researchers have hypothesized that attention difficulties in children are often misinterpreted by teachers as reflecting a diagnosis of ADHD. One study found that teachers identified almost 24 percent of their class as meeting criteria for one of the three subtypes of ADHD. Factors such as larger class sizes and student minority status were found to be responsible for some of these inaccurate identifications. It is our opinion that student support services professionals can best determine whether attention problems in the classroom are indicative of an attention disorder, another diagnosis, or related to maladaptive environments or circumstances.

Canadian and American medical practice guidelines state that medication is the first line of treatment for ADHD. However, both sets of practice guidelines support the value of educating patients, families, and teachers about ADHD, stating they are necessary additions to treatment. This is another area where student support professionals can be an instrumental part of the treatment plan.

There is a great variability in cognitive and behavioral responses to medication for attention disorders. Dosages of stimulants that are too large tend to have adverse side effects often described as the "zombie effect," including blunting of affect, sadness, and social withdrawal. At times, children and youth with ADHD are prescribed medication as a diagnostic tool, with only one trial without proper medication monitoring. This situation can result in diagnostic errors and inaccurate interpretation of response to medication.

School psychologists are in a key position to recommend referral for medication trials. They are able to determine the severity and type of symptoms, as well as parents' attitudes and potential for medication compliance. If students take medication, school psychologists can play an important role in monitoring the response to medication and making recommendations for additional intervention.

ANXIETY DISORDERS[3]

Anxiety disorders are one of the most common conditions exhibited by school-age children and youth and can interfere significantly with academic performance and success. Prevalence rates generally range from 2.6 to 20 percent with one meta-analysis showing the highest prevalence at 41.2 percent in a preadolescent sample. In a study surveying caseloads of primary care physicians the prevalence rate was as high as 17 percent. A separate study found that 72 percent of children identified with anxiety disorders had not received any counseling.

Separation Anxiety Disorder

One of the most common anxiety disorders is separation anxiety, seen most often in primary-level school children. The symptoms include excessive anxiety regarding separation from home or family members that can cause specific difficulties in academic, social, or other important areas of functioning. The child is often afraid that family members will become ill or die while he or she is at school.

Other anxiety symptoms include exhibiting severe homesickness and needing to be reunited with family members exceeding what is normally seen at the child's developmental stage. The prevalence of separation anxiety is estimated to be approximately 4 percent of children and young adolescents.

Generalized Anxiety Disorder

This variant of anxiety disorders includes children and adolescents who worry excessively over upcoming events and occurrences, such as academic performance, sport activities, being late for school, or natural disasters. These behaviors can occur without cause, such as a child who does well academically, but continues to be anxious about marks. Anxious students' academic progress can be affected by their tendency to lack confidence or be perfectionistic. The prevalence rate for separation anxiety in children and youth has been reported to be approximately 5 percent.

Social Phobia/Social Anxiety Disorder

This anxiety disorder involves children and youth who have an ongoing fear of public embarrassment, such as public speaking, performing, or simply being in social situations. Physical symptoms are produced by the anxious feelings, including tremors, palpitations, sweating, stomach upset, and can result in a panic attack. Some students attempt to cope with this anxiety by avoiding places or situations where these feelings previously occurred, such as school. The prevalence rate for social phobia/social anxiety disorder ranges from 3 to 13 percent.

Obsessive Compulsive Disorder

The student with this disorder needs to perform compulsive acts in order to respond to his or her own obsessive thoughts. Obsessions are thoughts, impulses, or mental images that are repeated, occur frequently, are intrusive, and cause severe anxiety or distress. Compulsions are behaviors that are often repeated such as a student constantly checking if he or she has the house key, frequent hand washing, or "hearing" an inner voice counting. Performing these acts reduces the stress the obsessions cause.

Obsessive compulsive disorder (OCD) is considered rare in children and youth, ranging from 0.2 to 0.8 percent in children and up to 2 percent in adolescents.

Post-traumatic Stress Disorder

Post-traumatic stress disorder (PTSD) occurs following exposure to traumatic events where an individual witnesses or is threatened with serious injury or death. PTSD also applies when an individual experiences serious injury. The student's response is characterized by intense fear, helplessness, or horror. These feelings are often expressed as severe agitation and can be reexperienced through repeated memories, expressions of the event in play, dreams of the event, or flashbacks.

There can be extreme distress when the student sees symbols that resemble the event, leading him or her to avoid stimuli that cause these associations to occur. Other symptoms include difficulty falling or staying asleep, irritability, angry outbursts, difficulty concentrating, hypervigilance, and an exaggerated startle response.

PTSD was once considered very rare in children and youth. This was due to the fact that the mental health community did not acknowledge that PTSD could be a childhood disorder. Nevertheless, prevalence rates for PTSD in children and youth vary widely, depending on the power of the stressors, the degree of exposure to the traumatic event, and the amount of time elapsed since the event.

One of the strongest predictors of having PTSD is previous exposure to mental health symptoms and trauma. Thus, children and youth who live in inner-city environments and are vulnerable to high rates of exposure to poverty, crime, drug use, and community violence are more likely to develop PTSD.

A study of over four thousand American youth aged twelve to seventeen found that 3.7 percent of boys and over 6 percent of girls reported PTSD symptoms in the previous six months. Another study examined data from a clinic treating refugee children. The children who came from war zones had a high rate of PTSD (63 percent). Schools today have students who are subject to or witness violence. In addition, urban schools are registering refugee claimants from war-torn countries who have witnessed or been themselves victims of genocidal acts.

In view of the nature of this particular diagnosis, we suggest that treatment in a familiar place, specifically their local school, may be more effective and less stressful for students than attending a community clinic or hospital.

MOOD DISORDERS[4]

There are two types of mood disorders in children and youth: depression and bipolar disorder. The overall prevalence rate for mood disorders ranges from 5 to 15 percent in children and adolescents.

Depression

Children and youth with depression exhibit a persistent and major loss of interest or pleasure in their usual activities, poor appetite and/or weight loss, and lack of sleep or too much sleep. As well, symptoms can include motor agitation or decreased activity levels, fatigue, mood swings, feelings of worthlessness and low self-esteem, guilt, diminished ability to concentrate, and sometimes suicidal ideation or suicide attempts. Other symptoms can include feelings of apathy, bleak outlooks, increased irritability, confusion, lack of motivation to do schoolwork, and general withdrawal. An additional category, dysthymia, involves chronic, low grade depressive symptoms leading to significant functional impairments.

Depression in children is often masked by what appear to be behavior problems. Depressed children can be agitated, hyperactive, silly, or simply withdrawn.

Studies in the United States and Canada reveal rates of depression in children under age fourteen of 1.1 to 3.5 percent and 5.6 to 8.3 percent in adolescents. Unrecognized and untreated, depression is the most common cause of suicide. Students with a sibling and/or a parent with depression have a 15 percent higher chance of developing depression.

A combination of biological and environmental causes can trigger depression. For example, stress brought on by family dysfunction, death of a relative or close friend, divorce, a move, or a learning disability have been cited as triggers of depressive episodes in some individuals. Clinical depression in adolescents is often underrecognized because of the commonly held belief that teenagers are normally moody and irritable.

Bipolar Disorder

Bipolar disorder occurs when the individual has episodes of mania and may also have depression. There can also be agitated depression, or dysphoric mania. Manic phases include elevation of mood, expansiveness, or irritability.

The prevalence rate for bipolar disorder in children and youth has risen dramatically in the last decade. This is thought to be mainly due to the change in definitions in the DSM-IV–TR. Reports show that in 1996, the prevalence in the United States of bipolar disorder in children was 1.3 per 10,000, whereas in 2004 the prevalence had increased to 73 per 10,000. Hospital-based diagnosis increased by four times for adolescents in these intervening years.

DISRUPTIVE DISORDERS: OPPOSITIONAL DEFIANT AND CONDUCT DISORDERS[5]

Oppositional defiant disorder (ODD) occurs when four or more of the following behaviors occur regularly: temper outbursts, arguing with adults, noncompliance, deliberately annoying others, blaming others, being easily annoyed, angry, resentful, spiteful, and vindictive. Behaviors of this nature are primarily directed toward authority figures such as teachers, administrators, and parents, but can also be directed toward peers.

Conduct disorder (CD) is characterized by three or more of the following behaviors: aggression to people or animals, destruction of property, stealing or lying, and severe rule violations. Levels of severity depend on the number and frequency of behaviors, and how much harm is done to others.

Prevalence rates for disruptive disorders overall range from 5.8 to 14.7 percent of children and youth for ODD or CD. The U.S. Surgeon General's Report on Mental Health reported prevalence rates ranging from 1 to 6 percent for ODD and 1 to 4 percent for CD (U.S. DHHS 1999).

Disruptive disorders often co-occur with depression, learning disabilities (LD), and/or ADHD, most often when these comorbid conditions are not diagnosed early or properly managed.

SLOW LEARNERS[6]

Slow learners are children whose intellectual functioning is below average but above the intellectually deficient level (scoring approximately at the 5th to 14th percentile on IQ tests). Their scores on academic tests are commensurate with their intellectual functioning. Their adaptive behavior (communication, daily living skills, and socialization skills) is within the broad average range. Slow learners compose almost 15 percent of the student population.

Research has discerned that over 70 percent of high school dropouts can be classified as slow learners. These students cannot succeed in a regular class without a modified academic program. However, they are often not eligible for special education support because they do not meet certain diagnostic criteria. Children and youth who are slow learners are sometimes diagnosed with anxiety and depression.

SPEECH AND LANGUAGE DISORDERS[7]

Speech and language disorders include expressive language disorders, such as limited vocabulary, difficulty recalling words, grammar and syntax difficulties, and delayed communication. Receptive language disorders involve difficulty understanding words and sentences. Speech disorders involve difficulties articulating words. Stuttering is also frequently found in school-aged children. These conditions can co-occur with other disorders such as learning disabilities, acquired brain injury, or pervasive developmental disorders.

Speech and language disorders are fairly common in young children. It is estimated that 7 percent of kindergarten-age students have specific language impairments and that sixteen of every one thousand children are estimated to have a chronic speech disorder. It is estimated that 4 percent of six-year-olds have a specific language impairment.

The DSM-IV–TR lists several types of speech and language problems. Expressive language disorders are reported to have a prevalence rate ranging from 3 to 7 percent in school-age children. Mixed receptive-expressive language disorders have a prevalence rate of approximately 3 percent, but it is generally less common than expressive language disorder. Phonological and stuttering disorders account for a prevalence rate of 0.5 percent and 0.8 percent in school-age children.

Research has revealed that approximately 50 percent of child psychiatric referrals have language difficulties. Researchers concluded that students with speech and language disorders are vulnerable to emotional disorder as early as school entry; they not only require language intervention, but possibly social and emotional support. These studies found improved outcomes in adolescents when speech and language difficulties were addressed and resolved.

DEVELOPMENTAL DISABILITIES[8]

Developmental disabilities are diagnosed in students who have below average intellectual functioning, generally below the 2nd percentile. In addition, these students have impaired adaptive functioning in at least two of the following areas: communication, daily living skills, socialization, and academics. Developmental disabilities are generally classified into four levels determined by the IQ score: mild, moderate, severe, and profound.

The prevalence rates for developmental disabilities range between 0.8 to 1.2 percent for the mild range, and from 0.3 to 0.5 percent for the severe range. There is a four- to fivefold increase in prevalence of psychiatric disorders in children with developmental disabilities in comparison with the nondisabled childhood population.

AUTISM SPECTRUM DISORDERS[9]

Autism spectrum disorders (ASD) refers to a number of specific disorders. Autistic disorder is characterized by severe impairments in three areas of functioning that begins before age three. The first area of impairment involves maladaptive social functioning, characterized by poor eye contact and atypical facial expressions and gestures. Consequently, social relationships do not develop normally.

The second area of impairment is communication skills. This is characterized by oral language delays or complete lack of oral language, stereotyped use of language such as echoing (echolalia), and a lack of developmentally appropriate social communication.

The third area of impairment includes repetitive and stereotyped motor behaviors (e.g., hand flapping), preoccupation with certain objects, narrow interests, difficulty with transitions, and inability to change certain routines or rituals.

Asperger's syndrome is a disorder on the autism spectrum characterized by impairment in social interaction and by stereotyped behavior patterns, interests, or activities. In this case, there is no clinically significant delay in language, cognitive development, or adaptive behavior, except in the development of social skills.

Rhett's disorder and childhood disintegrative disorder are rare autism spectrum disorders. In both diagnoses, normal developmental progression stops early in childhood. Previously acquired social, motor, communication, and cognitive skills are lost.

Pervasive developmental disorder not otherwise specified (PDD-NOS) is a diagnostic category of autism spectrum disorders. This diagnosis is made when a child or youth meets some, but not all, of the diagnostic criteria for autism spectrum disorders. There must also be significant impairments in functioning.

Prevalence rates for autism spectrum disorders overall range from 0.02 to 0.62 percent. An international study revealed the following prevalence rates per 10,000 children: 13 for autistic disorder, 21 for pervasive developmental disorder not otherwise specified, and 2.6 for Asperger's disorder. The prevalence rate for childhood disintegrative disorder is 2 per 100,000 children. The estimate for the prevalence for all autistic disorders is 0.6 percent.

There is a popular belief that autism spectrum disorders are increasing at an epidemic rate. Research has revealed an elevenfold increase in autism prevalence rates in the previous decade. However, these researchers, and others, believe that the addition of Asperger's syndrome into prevalence statistics, earlier identification, and improvement in diagnostic criteria and methodology have been the major contributors to this increase.

Comorbidity in pervasive developmental disorders has been studied extensively. In a sample of children diagnosed with PDD-NOS, 80.6 percent had at least one other psychiatric diagnosis.

BARRIERS TO LEARNING LESS COMMONLY REFERRED FOR INTERVENTION AT SCHOOL

TIC DISORDERS[10]

Tic disorders include a variety of difficulties characterized by motor or vocal tics. A tic is a sudden, quick stereotyped physical movement (e.g., head twitching) or vocalization (e.g., throat clearing). Tourette's disorder occurs when multiple motor and vocal tics are exhibited many times a day usually in bouts. These symptoms can contribute to impairments in social and academic functioning. Tics are often comorbid with other childhood mental health or learning disorders.

The DSM-IV-TR states that the prevalence rate for Tourette's is higher in children than adults, ranging from 5 to 30 per 10,000.

PRENATAL MATERNAL SUBSTANCE ABUSE[11]

There are well-known negative physical effects on the developing fetus when pregnant women abuse substances. There are also negative effects on a child's development when their caregivers abuse substances. Prevalence rates for both legal and illegal substance substances use during pregnancy have been estimated as follows. Approximately 10 percent of pregnant women use alcohol, 20 percent smoke cigarettes, 10 percent use marijuana, 1 percent use cocaine, and 0.5 percent use opiates.

One area of prenatal maternal substance abuse that has been studied to a great extent is the effects of alcohol use during pregnancy. Fetal alcohol spectrum disorder (FASD) is now referred to as a spectrum because damage can range from mild to severe. This spectrum includes, but is not limited to, fetal alcohol syndrome (FAS), partial fetal alcohol syndrome (pFAS), alcohol-related neurodevelopmental disorder (ARND), and alcohol-related birth defects (ARBD).

There are four criteria required for the diagnosis of FAS: confirmed maternal drinking during pregnancy, growth retardation, facial anomalies, and brain damage. There are often congenital defects of the heart and other organs, central nervous system dysfunction, and head, facial, and physical abnormalities. Other indicators include developmental and motor delays, hyperactivity, learning and attention problems, and a lower IQ.

ARND is diagnosed when there are only signs of central nervous system and cognitive abnormalities without the other criteria, aside from confirmed exposure to alcohol *in utero*. The central nervous system effects are manifested by learning and behavior problems in school.

It is difficult to estimate the prevalence of FASD because many of these children are misdiagnosed, or not diagnosed at all. In addition, prevalence appears to differ among populations. Prevalence rates vary from 0.21 to 0.9 per 1,000 births. FASDs account for approximately 5 percent of congenital anomalies and 10 to 20 percent of cases of mild mental retardation.

Outcome studies reveal that only about 30 percent of children with FAS were living with their mothers during their teenage years. Over 86 percent of children who remained at home with their mothers were involved with child protection services for neglect and 52 percent for child abuse.

EATING DISORDERS[12]

Eating disorders such as anorexia nervosa and bulimia are most commonly diagnosed during adolescence. Anorexia nervosa is defined by the inability to maintain weight above 85 percent of normal body weight. Individuals with this disorder are exceedingly fearful of gaining weight and have an extremely distorted body image, believing they are overweight when in fact they are severely underweight.

Bulimia involves binge eating where the individual consumes more than a normal amount of food in a certain period of time. The individual lacks control over the ability to stop eating. This behavior is followed by purging (self-induced vomiting or excessive use of laxatives), excessive exercise, or fasting.

Binge eating is a newly recognized disorder that involves episodic uncontrolled eating without vomiting or laxative use.

The Surgeon General's report stated that approximately 3 percent of young women have one of the three main eating disorders. The following gender-based prevalence rates have been reported: 0.7 percent of girls and 0.2 percent of boys for anorexia, and 1.2 percent of girls and 0.4 percent for boys for bulimia nervosa. Canadian data revealed an overall prevalence rate of 0.1 percent.

SELECTIVE MUTISM[13]

Selective mutism is a disorder where children do not speak in social situations, especially at school, but they do speak at home. Estimates of prevalence rates range from 0.18 to 0.72 percent, and this disorder is often grouped in with anxiety disorders.

SENSORY DISORDERS: BLIND AND LOW VISION AND DEAF AND
HARD-OF-HEARING[14]

The prevalence rate for blind and low vision students has been estimated
to be 0.16 percent. Approximately 10 to 15 percent of children fail hearing screenings at school, although the majority have transient conductive
hearing losses from otitis media. Hearing disorders are estimated to have a
prevalence rate of 1.3 percent.

Most students with hearing and vision difficulties do well in school,
some with assistance from specialized teachers. However, some may require
intervention from support services professionals when they experience
school-adjustment problems or additional difficulties, such as learning disabilities or mental health issues.

CHRONIC AND LIFE-THREATENING ILLNESSES[15]

Advances in medicine and technology have resulted in more children who
have chronic or life-threatening illnesses attending school for longer periods
of time. Diagnoses in this category can include childhood cancer, sickle-cell
anemia, asthma, and diabetes.

Prevalence rates for childhood cancer are generally below 1 percent.
Approximately 20 percent of schoolchildren have some type of chronic
medical condition. The majority of these children are able to cope well in
school. However, about 40 percent of these children do experience school-
related problems.

IDEAS TO CONSIDER

- Prevalence data suggest that the numbers of students facing different
  biological-psychological barriers to learning in classrooms can vary
  and be substantial.
- When a student is not achieving, or not behaving appropriately, it
  is important to determine if biological-psychological barriers to learning exist.
- Determining the presence and extent of co-occurring mental health
  issues is important when addressing barriers that are more academic
  in nature (e.g., learning disabilities, slow learners).

3

ENVIRONMENTAL-CIRCUMSTANTIAL BARRIERS TO LEARNING

When students experience difficulties, more consideration should be given to environmental-circumstantial barriers to learning as contributing factors. We present examples of these barriers below. Each barrier is defined and prevalence rates are given, as well as how some of these barriers manifest in the classroom.

BARRIERS TO LEARNING COMMONLY REFERRED FOR INTERVENTION AT SCHOOL: SOME EXAMPLES

CHILDREN AND YOUTH EXPOSED TO DOMESTIC VIOLENCE[1]

A study in a U.S. county found that children and youth were present in almost half of domestic violence events investigated by the police. In a nationally representative sample of eight thousand U.S. residents, 25 percent of women and 7.6 percent of men reported a lifetime prevalence of extreme violence by a spouse or partner.

Children's exposure to domestic violence can result in post-traumatic stress disorder, other anxiety disorders, depression, and overall behavior problems. One study examined over one thousand children eight to sixteen years old who were in community-based programs for children exposed to domestic violence. Eighteen percent of the sample showed evidence of externalizing behaviors (e.g., noncompliance, temper outbursts), while 13 percent met criteria for internalizing (e.g., withdrawal, low mood) behaviors.

Children exposed to domestic violence were more likely to have difficulties in school, score lower on tests, exhibit aggressive and antisocial behavior, as well as be depressed, anxious, and show slower cognitive development. Boys exposed to violence as children were more likely to engage in violence, while girls were more likely to be victims of violence later in life. It is important to determine whether the child's exposure to domestic violence is also occurring with child abuse itself.

CHILD ABUSE[2]

There are four types of child abuse: physical, emotional, sexual, and neglect. Experiencing child abuse can adversely affect many area of functioning, currently and in the future. The degree of impact largely depends on the nature and severity of the mistreatment, how long it had been occurring before disclosure or discovery, and on the timing and quality of professional resources available to treat the victimized individual.

Although many cases of child abuse remain undisclosed, the United States National Longitudinal Study of Adolescent Health used self-reports and found the following prevalence rates. Supervision neglect was most prevalent at 41.5 percent, while physical assault was reported to be 28.4 percent, physical neglect was reported to be 11.8 percent, and sexual abuse was reported to be 4.5 percent. Recent Canadian statistics revealed that over 25 percent of sexual abuse cases occurred with other forms of child abuse.

Abused children can experience poor physical health and mental health disorders. There can also be many negative behavioral outcomes, such as teen pregnancy, substance abuse, violence, and other criminal activities. Furthermore, cognitive dysfunction has been linked with child abuse, including deficits in attention, abstract reasoning, language development, and problem-solving skills.

CHANGE IN FAMILY CONSTITUTION[3]

Change in family constitution includes separation and divorce, long-term parental absence, and death of a parent or caregiver. Recent statistics reveal that approximately one in two marriages ends in divorce. Marital conflicts that often lead to divorce have the following effects on children: an increase in internalizing behaviors, (e.g., withdrawal and depression) and externalizing behaviors (e.g., aggression). Although children in stepfamilies have been shown to have higher rates of behavior problems, it may well be that stepfamilies can amplify problems already established in the original family members.

SOCIAL DISCRIMINATION[4]

Although society values and promotes diversity, outcomes for diverse children and youth may not always reflect this point of view. For example, these students can experience discrimination and diminished opportunities (including lack of resources). These situations in themselves can be the underlying cause of some students' behavior difficulties. Moreover, these negative outcomes can sometimes be exacerbated by their family's mistrust of systems stemming from the discrimination they themselves experienced.

ECONOMIC CHALLENGES[5]

In 2007, the United Nations Children's Fund reported that approximately 21.9 percent of children in the United States under the age of eighteen years lived below the federally established poverty line. The prevalence rate in Canada was reported at 14.9 percent.

The materially and socially deprived conditions inherent in poverty affect quality of life as well as the physical, intellectual, emotional, and social development of children and youth. Studies have shown effects that include externalizing and internalizing symptoms, psychiatric symptoms, physical health issues, and deviant behavioral outcomes including teenage pregnancy, legal problems, substance abuse, and school dropout in both adolescents and, in some findings, younger children.

LOSS OF JOB/UNEMPLOYMENT[6]

Unemployment places stress on both parents and their children. Parental job loss and unemployment put children and youth at higher risk for behavioral and emotional challenges. A study of four hundred children whose parents were unemployed during the previous twelve months found that 18.6 percent met high risk criteria for behavioral and emotional problems.

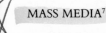

MASS MEDIA[7]

It is our opinion that the negative influence of mass media can be considered an environmental-circumstantial barrier to learning.

The Kaiser Family Foundation surveyed over one thousand parents of children age two to seventeen with respect to their understanding of mass media and children and youth. Sixty-six percent of parents were sufficiently concerned with the amount of sex, violence, and adult language in the media that they favored government intervention in media control. Also of key interest in this study is that despite their expressed concern, most parents seemed to believe that their own children were not exposed to a significant amount of inappropriate content.

There are three possible recent changes in the home environment that explains parents' lack of concern with their children's mass media consumption.

1. Parents are more aware of potential negative effects of mass media and therefore may be making more of an effort at choosing appropriate media for their children.
2. Parents' concept of what is deemed "inappropriate" has changed, allowing for a broader acceptance of media selection that would have at one time been considered morally questionable or unacceptable for children's viewing.
3. Parents may not have a "real handle" on what their children are viewing.

Another Kaiser Family Foundation study found that children's bedrooms are becoming "multi-media centres." Percentages of children and youth eight to eighteen years old with media found in the bedrooms included:

- 66 percent had televisions
- 54 percent had VCR or DVD players
- 49 percent had video game players
- 31 percent had computers
- 20 percent had Internet access

The Kaiser Foundation study also indicated that a majority of eight- to eighteen-year-olds report that their parents have no rules about television watching and if they do, only 20 percent of them enforce the rule "most" of the time. Furthermore, this age group spends an average of 6.5 hours a day connected with media, which is more time per day than they spend in the classroom. Also worthy of note is that three out of four children spend on average only forty-three minutes a day reading for pleasure.

Recent research on television viewing found that 75 percent of children watched over two hours, 33 percent watched for more than four hours on weeknights. By age eighteen, it was determined that the average child watched twenty-eight hours of television a week, which included 16,000 simulated murders. Childhood exposure to media violence is associated with increased aggressive behavior and attitudes, desensitization to real and fantasy violence, and increased depression, nightmares, and sleep disturbance.

BARRIERS TO LEARNING AND LABELING[8]

Biological-psychological barriers to learning can overlap with environmental-circumstantial barriers resulting in complex cases that become difficult to diagnose or treat. In Ms. W.'s and Mr. M.'s classes, we find a number of students who have barriers to learning in both areas. For example, Carl in Ms. W.'s class has a diagnosis of ADHD. The treatment for his particular diagnosis is further complicated by his recent move into a shelter with his mother and brother because of domestic violence on the part of his father. Evan, in Mr. M.'s class, was diagnosed early with a biological-psychological barrier to learning (a learning disability); however, his parents refusal (environmental-circumstantial barrier to learning) to accept the diagnosis prevented him from accessing the intervention he required.

There is often a propensity to rely on discrete diagnoses when addressing certain behavior and emotional difficulties in students. Students with complex conditions like Carl and Evan require investigation of both biological-psychological and environmental-circumstantial barriers to learning as a means of identifying and planning treatment for their difficulties. Therefore, before labeling these students with individual pathologies, it is best to determine whether the nature of a student's difficulties are biological-psychological, environmental-circumstantial or both.

The propensity to refer primarily individual cases to school-based support services (often to access special education) can result in the following negative systemic effects.

- School-based support professionals serve only a small proportion of high-needs students.
- Waiting lists for services increase and often remain at high levels.
- Students at risk for problems or at the early stages of challenging behavior do not receive service.

The reliance on referring individual cases may well be linked to the tendency to base students' problems on individual factors (i.e., biological-psychological barriers to learning). This practice can lead to misdiagnoses and ineffective interventions.

LOOK UP! Adelman and Taylor have studied school-based mental health issues extensively. They state that students' everyday problems are often translated into psychiatric symptoms. According to these researchers, psychiatric labels are often overused, when in reality these labels are the consequences of untreated or undertreated learning problems. They call for a change from perceiving many student problems as person-centered pathology to understanding them as possibly being linked with socioeconomic and sociocultural problems.

Many school systems are structured to address discrete student problems with categorical programs (e.g., special education placement determined by psychological assessment). There are limited structures available to address environmental-circumstantial barriers with universal and targeted prevention programs. It is difficult to address students facing environmental-circumstantial barriers to learning when school systems are structured in this manner.

The costs of using primarily categorical approaches to addressing student difficulties is sizable, when most supports continue to be utilized for high-needs students. The implementation of Response to Intervention is beginning to address this problem, as discussed in chapters 6 and 7.

IDEAS TO CONSIDER

- Environmental-circumstantial barriers to learning are less often considered when students are experiencing difficulties.
- Prevalence data suggest that the numbers of students facing environmental-circumstantial barriers to learning in classrooms can vary and be substantial.
- Exposure and usage of mass media can be considered an environmental-circumstantial barrier to learning.
- Students' problems are often attributed to individual pathology; investigation of both biological-psychological and environmental-circumstantial barriers to learning is essential in identifying and planning intervention for students with difficulties.

SEE VISUAL P. 4

4

NEGATIVE OUTCOMES OF INADEQUATE INTERVENTION FOR BARRIERS TO LEARNING

Negative outcomes can result when students receive inadequate intervention to address their barriers to learning (see figure 1.1 in chapter 1). We provide prevalence data on some examples of these negative outcomes. We also propose a hypothetical negative outcome that can also affect these students' classmates.

Inadequate intervention refers to

- Inappropriate intervention due to
  - lack of mental health intervention by appropriate professionals
  - academic-focused solutions to mental health problems
- Ineffective interventions, such as
  - student is facing biological-psychological barriers but is not diagnosed or is misdiagnosed
  - student is facing environmental-circumstantial barriers, but problems are attributed to individual pathology
- Intervention is appropriate but insufficient in duration or too narrow in scope to be effective   MHO₄
- Lack of intervention due to factors such as stigma, long waiting lists, and limited resources

The following section is not an exhaustive list of negative outcomes of inadequate intervention for barriers to learning. The section includes some key examples: bullying, school refusal, early school leaving (dropping out), addictive behavior (substance abuse and gambling), suicide ideation, suicide, and school violence.

NEGATIVE OUTCOMES

BULLYING[1]

Olweus defined *bullying* as negative physical or verbal actions (1993). These actions are intended to cause fear and distress in the victim, are repeated over time, and have a clear power differential between the bully and the victim. Bullying can be direct, as in physical or verbal bullying, or indirect as in gossiping about students or excluding students. Bullies and their victims are both at risk for maladaptive relationships with parents and peers as well as social and emotional difficulties.

Bullying is not something that some children simply "do" and "grow out of." Research studies have found that some students only bully during early school years, some stop by the end of high school, and others continue into adulthood. Bullying has also been found to be related to negative behaviors in later life, including sexual harassment, dating aggression, workplace harassment, marital aggression, and elder abuse.

Parents and teachers are not often aware of the extent of bullying activities. A study of children in grades 4 and 5 revealed that over half of the children's teachers and parents were not aware that the students were bullied. Students often related that telling an adult made bullying worse. Interestingly, most teachers mentioned that they lacked both sufficient time and resources to properly deal with bullying while also trying to cover the curriculum.

Prevalence rates of bullying mostly consist of self-report data in surveys, which often overestimates numbers. Nevertheless, the numbers are sufficiently high to make it clear that bullying is a pervasive problem in schools. A Canadian survey of youth in grades 7 to 12 found that over one-quarter (27.3 percent) of students reported that they had bullied students at school, while 30.9 percent reported being victims of bullying. A similar Canadian survey of younger students in grades 1 to 6 found that 27 percent experienced both physical and verbal bullying.

Recently, cyberbullying has been added to the bully's arsenal. Utilizing electronic communication is very attractive to bullies because of relative anonymity, availability twenty-four hours a day through the Internet and cell phones, and the potential vastness of the audience. In addition, the use of cell phones cameras to capture embarrassing situations and sending them out on video clips to peers or posting them on social networking sites are other acts with potentially grave consequences for the victim.

Prevalence data on cyberbullying is just beginning to be collected. A survey of over 1,200 late elementary and early high school students in the

Netherlands found that 23 percent reported being victims of cyberbullying. Parents of these students reported that they were not particularly aware of the bullying and underestimated their own children's bullying behavior.

A U.S. survey of four thousand grade 6 to 8 students found just over one-tenth (11 percent) had been victims of cyberbullying at least once in the last few months. Four percent indicated they had bullied someone electronically in the past few months and 7 percent indicated that they had been both bullied and victimized electronically.

There are several approaches available to address bullying behavior. In the past, this behavior was often addressed through conflict resolution with the parties immediately involved. The victim is often referred for individual counseling and the bully receives consequences. Although this approach can be effective, general practice favors involving the whole school in a wide range of antibullying activities.   TIER 1

School districts are increasingly using a schoolwide approach as an antibullying strategy that is more preventative in nature. This type of approach reaches the bullies, the victims, and the bystanders and also involves the whole school community, addressing bullying while promoting positive behavioral supports.

SCHOOL REFUSAL[2]

Truancy originally referred to students who simply refused to attend school. However, the term *school refusal* includes a broader range of students with specific reasons for not attending school. Students who are bullied and have school phobia sometimes refuse to attend school. In addition, some students who are diagnosed with social phobias and anxiety have difficulty attending school.

School refusal prevalence rates range from 5 to 28 percent. These wide prevalence rates are related to the lack of consensus among researchers about definitions and classifications of school refusal.

It is important to provide a comprehensive multidisciplinary assessment of all school refusal behavior. School refusal is symptomatic of a larger problem in the student's life. These larger problems can include homelessness, poverty, teenage pregnancy, school violence and victimization, negative school climate, poor school connectedness and disengagement, large amounts of unsupervised out of school time, inadequate parental involvement, low levels of parent education, and other negative family variables.

EARLY SCHOOL LEAVING/DROPOUTS[3]

Even though there is no standard method of measuring graduation rates, it is conservatively estimated that between 10 to 15 percent of students in the United States do not graduate from high school. Researchers speculate that these numbers are underestimates and are higher for students from low income families, racial minorities (two to four times higher), and students with disabilities (up to five times higher).

In some large city school systems in the United States, the drop-out rate has been measured as high as 50 percent. Canadian statistics show that nationally, about 10 percent of students do not complete high school with prevalence disparities in gender, race, and region.

There are warning signs for early school leaving that increase chances of dropping out. These factors have been studied extensively. Researchers have identified "signals" as early as middle grades that increase chances of dropping out. Students with one or more of the following risk factors were 75 percent more likely to dropout of high school: failing marks in English and mathematics, poor attendance, and poor class behavior.

It is therefore important to build in schoolwide prevention programs in early grades to promote school connectedness, provide positive behavior supports, and identify potential problems early.

ADDICTIONS[4]

Substance Abuse

In the United States, the Surgeon General's Report on Mental Health stated that the most relevant issue in youth substance abuse is the co-occurrence of substance abuse disorders with other mental health disorders. It was reported that 41 to 65 percent of all individuals (not just youth) with lifetime substance abuse disorders also have a lifetime history of mental health disorders, with the highest rates in the fifteen- to twenty-four-year-old age group. Gender-based prevalence rates more reflective of school-aged children and youth (age twelve to seventeen) in the United States was reported to be 8.2 percent for boys and 6.2 percent for girls (U.S. DHHS 1999).

A Canadian provincial study in 2007 of students in grades 7 to 12 determined that although rates of substance abuse in this population have decreased, it is still substantially high. Alcohol use is the most commonly abused substance, with 61 percent of students stating that they have used alcohol in the past twelve months. Cannabis was the next highest substance abused, at

26 percent. Nonmedical use of pain relievers was next at 21 percent, while fourth in prevalence was cigarette smoking, at 12 percent. Thirty-one percent indicated that someone had tried to sell them drugs at school.

Gambling

The prevalence rate for gambling in students in grades 7 to 12 was determined to be 4.5 percent in a Canadian provincial survey. More than five types of gambling activities were reported by 5.9 percent of students in the last year. Activities included cards, lottery tickets, sports pools, dice, bingo, sports lottery tickets, video gambling machines, Internet gambling, and attending casinos.

A commonly discussed theory in addictions is that youth with addictive behaviors are attempting to deal with their untreated mental health disorders. Surveys support this hypothesis. In the Canadian survey mentioned above, 9 percent of grade 7 to 12 students surveyed indicated both hazardous levels of drinking and psychological stresses including anxiety and depression. It also appears rare that students receive treatment for addictive behaviors. In the same survey, only 1.5 percent of students indicated that they had received treatment for a drug problem.

When students are referred to community organizations for addiction treatment, it is important to involve school-based student support professionals, particularly for those students with concurrent mental health disorders. It is important to have a clear understanding of all barriers to learning these students may be experiencing. School-based professionals play a key role in integrating this information into treatment plans. In addition, more preventative approaches to address addiction issues are needed. It is essential that these educational programs be schoolwide and ongoing.

SUICIDE[5]

It is not unusual for some adolescents to have thoughts of suicide. Various surveys in both Canada and the United States have found prevalence of suicide ideation to range from 16.9 to 23.3 percent of adolescents. The prevalence rates for attempted suicide range from 3.1 to 15 percent of adolescents.

These prevalence rates are reflections of what the students themselves indicated on the surveys. It is well known that self-responder rates tend to be higher than other methods; however, it is important to note that such a high percentage of adolescents felt compelled to report this behavior.

Regardless of the prevalence rates, suicide is one of the leading causes of death among young people. Most successful suicides have a history of psychiatric disorders, particularly depression, and researchers all call for early recognition and treatment of these disorders in youth as one of the best preventative procedures.

Poor parental relationships, and not poor peer relationships, were associated with suicidal ideation and attempts among a national Canadian sample of twelve- and thirteen-year-olds and a sample of adolescents. Both studies supported early interventions, such as improving maladaptive parent-child relationships as important measures for preventing these behaviors in children and youth.

YOUTH VIOLENCE[6]

Poverty, racism, and untreated mental health disorders have been identified as the factors contributing to youth violence. A Canadian provincial government report linked these factors with the limited availability of programs for health and mental health promotion, as well as early identification and treatment provided in the context of youth's homes and schools. Youth violence is more likely to occur in a public place, and guns are more likely to be used as weapons.

Canadian survey data reveal that 19.5 percent of sampled youth reported that they had performed a violent act in the last twelve months. In addition, 28 percent of youth fifteen years of age and under were victims of violence in the last year.

U.S. survey data reveal that the percentage of high school students indicating they had been in physical fights in the last year was 33.2 percent, and 17.4 percent indicated they had carried some type of weapon in the past month. Just over 5 percent of youth aged twelve to nineteen reported being victims of violent crime during the year.

Substantial research has made connections between youth in jails and school-based problems. Studies report that a significant number of incarcerated youth had been expelled from school at some point, 70 percent have depressive symptoms, and 10 percent reported suicidal ideation. In addition, 33 percent had special education needs, specifically academic underachievement, and 66 percent came from one-parent families. These studies report that 40 to 70 percent of youth who are incarcerated are suspected of having undiagnosed and untreated mental health disorders.

In addition, schools that lack staff trained to address multi-need student populations may experience higher rates of violent youth behavior.

Research has shown that the development of antisocial and violent behaviors tends to move along predictable pathways, supporting early intervention activities as a means of preventing violent behavior in troubled children and youth.

THE MULTI-RIPPLE EFFECT[7]

The previous section identified some examples of negative outcomes from inadequate intervention of barriers to learning. We propose that there is one additional negative outcome of inadequate intervention of barriers to learning that can affect students *not* facing barriers to learning.

The research literature reveals a clear relationship between mental health difficulties and poor academic outcomes. We propose that students not facing barriers to learning may also have their academic progress compromised, adding an additional negative outcome to inadequately addressed barriers to learning.

This notion has been discussed in the school-based mental health literature. Rones and Hoagwood state that when students' mental health difficulties are not properly addressed, these students will not be able to adequately learn and benefit from the school environment. The authors also state that these students can have a negative influence on their classmates' social and academic environment. In classrooms, when students disrupt lessons, learning and teaching are compromised (2000).

We have developed the concept of the Multi-Ripple Effect to reflect the hypothetical impact on classmates' functioning from the behavior of students whose barriers to learning are inadequately addressed. This may result in the development of inappropriate classroom behaviors in students not facing barriers to learning.

We illustrated the Multi-Ripple Effect in the fictional classrooms of Ms. W. and Mr. M. There are several points of origin for the ripples, namely, each student with barriers to learning that are not being addressed. As the ripples disperse and reverberate throughout the classroom, a Multi-Ripple Effect ensues, with the resulting dynamics further compromising students' learning as well as teaching.

We have graphically represented the Multi-Ripple Effect in figures 4.1 and 4.2. The teacher is at the top of a grid of circles. Clear circles represent students not facing barriers. Differently shaded circles represent the students who are facing barriers to learning that were presented in Ms. W.'s (figure 4.1) and Mr. M.'s (figure 4.2) classes.

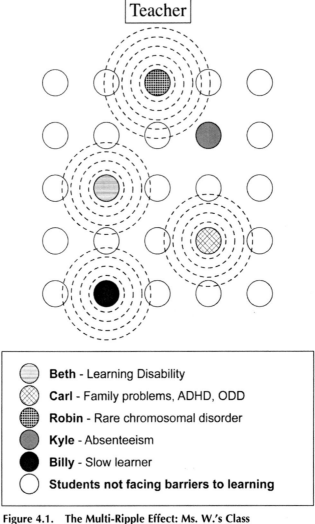

Figure 4.1.   The Multi-Ripple Effect: Ms. W.'s Class

The potential effects of these students' behaviors on classmates are represented by the dashed "ripples" that spread over some of the clear circles. As can be seen, the ripples intersect and reach some students in the class who would not normally be facing barriers to learning, like Rashid and Jamie in Ms. W.'s class.

We again caution the reader that the Multi-Ripple Effect is speculative. The number of students with problems and wide-ranging conse-

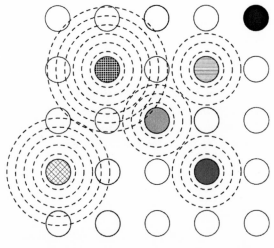

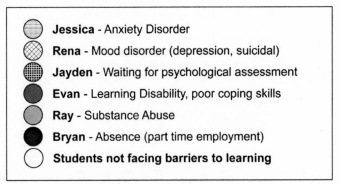

Figure 4.2.   The Multi-Ripple Effect: Mr. M.'s Class

quences on teaching and learning are exaggerated to illustrate the potential effects of not adequately addressing barriers to learning.

Barriers to learning also have an effect on teaching. Paternité and Johnston, two researchers in school-based mental health, provide a hypothetical example of the Multi-Ripple Effect, specifically with respect to teacher time dealing with behavioral disruptions. They hypothesized that teachers spend 204 hours or approximately thirty-four school days in an academic year dealing with disruptive behavior (2005). This would clearly have an effect on the disruptive students' classmates, if only from the missed teaching time.

We hypothesize that one of the reasons for teacher attrition may be related to inadequately addressed barriers to learning. Research examining the attrition rates of teachers determined that 10 percent of all new teachers resign prior to the end of the first year, 35 percent by the end of their third year, and nearly 50 percent by the end of five years.

In a recent survey, teachers (especially first year teachers) requested professional development when asked what they required for classroom management. Teachers at all levels of experience requested professional development to learn methods to ensure that student's negative behaviors are not a continuing distraction to teachers and students. The teachers asked for training to ensure student safety in the classroom and training in behavioral needs. Discipline problems stemming from challenging behaviors in schools are reported to be the main source of stress and burnout for educators.

We caution that the Multi-Ripple Effect is not indicative of a teacher's ability to manage his or her classroom or of the administrator's ability to manage the school. We hypothesize that the degree to which the Multi-Ripple Effect compromises learning and teaching may depend on the number, the nature, and the severity of students facing barriers to learning and whether they are receiving appropriate intervention for these barriers.

IDEAS TO CONSIDER

- In some situations, certain maladaptive behaviors and conditions (e.g., youth violence, bullying) are negative outcomes of inadequately addressed barriers to learning.
- Prevalence data for the negative outcomes suggest that these negative outcomes may be present in many classrooms and can be substantial.
- The Multi-Ripple Effect is a hypothetical negative outcome affecting some classmates of students facing barriers to learning.
- Learning can be compromised for students in the classroom who are not facing barriers to learning as a result of the Multi-Ripple Effect.
- The Multi-Ripple Effect may also compromise teaching.

5

EDUCATION AND MENTAL
HEALTH SYSTEM REFORMS
AND BARRIERS TO LEARNING

Education and mental health services are two systems that have a long
history of intense scrutiny by policy makers and funding systems. Both
the education and mental health systems are often subject to reports of un-
derfunding as well as wavering public confidence and support.

In the education system, policies have recently been driven by the goal
of improving student achievement along with increased accountability, for
example, the No Child Left Behind Act (NCLB) in the United States. In
Canada, similar legislation has recently been developed to improve student
achievement. Some of the initiatives include the implementation of large-
scale testing and supporting improvements in leadership and pedagogy.

The mental health field has similarly been subject to scrutiny by
policy makers and funding systems. Mental health services, particularly for
children and youth, are widely known to be fragmented and in need of
integration to produce better outcomes.

EDUCATION REFORM AND BARRIERS TO LEARNING[1]

Barriers to learning are discussed at length in many disciplines, most notably
education reform. Education reform, in this instance, refers to methods to
increase school achievement levels (especially in schools that have either stag-
nant or falling levels of achievement on test scores) and closing the "achievement gap," which refers to consistently lower test scores for students with
special needs when compared to the rest of the school population.

A full discussion on this area of educational reform is beyond the scope
of this book; however, it is important to briefly review this area of the
literature in order to support the integrated school-based support services

approach to prevention, reduction, and management of barriers to student learning.

In the education reform literature, barriers to learning are often not clearly delineated. These barriers are mentioned primarily in discussions regarding disadvantaged students or those who for various reasons are seen as unable to achieve (e.g., poverty, learning disabilities, low cognitive functioning, family challenges, chronic illnesses).

Research has shown that certain school-based factors do influence academic outcomes. For example, small school sizes, emphasis on academic skills with respect to teacher pedagogy, and learning strategies and academic supports that are highly adaptable have been shown to increase attendance, test scores, and graduation rates.

Administrator-based factors have also been found to influence academic outcomes. For example, developing caring school environments and increasing student, teacher, and family cooperation can result in increased student achievement. In addition, when school leaders focus on academic achievement, provide appropriate supports, and retain high academic expectations, schools perform better academically.

Leaders in education reform, such as Fullan, Hill, and Crévola (2006), Hargreaves and Shirley (2009), and Blankstein (2004), promote improvements in school leadership and pedagogy to increase student achievement. They also support partnerships with community-based services to improve education outcomes for students facing barriers to learning.

Barriers to learning, specifically those involving mental health, should be included more often in discussions of education reforms. The role of school-based mental health professionals also needs to be included in these discussions. These professionals can play a significant role in increasing student achievement.

Adelman and Taylor, in their work at the UCLA Center for Mental Health in Schools, state that good instruction from excellent teachers alone cannot ensure all students succeed at school. In schools where there are a high proportion of barriers to learning (such as learning disabilities, untreated and unrecognized mental health problems, poverty, high crime, poor parent engagement, and so on), any initial increases in test scores tend to plateau after a few years (Center for Mental Health 2008b).

Adelman and Taylor clearly state that in school improvement planning literature, the essential piece that is missing is addressing barriers to learning and teaching. Efforts to address these barriers are marginalized because they are not mandated by governing bodies, and therefore are not included in education goals. Improved instruction through the context of improved leadership is understandably essential, although these authors state that it is insufficient to achieve full education reform.

The researchers at the Center for Mental Health in Schools state that this inconsistent progress is due to schools marginalizing services to address nonacademic barriers to learning and teaching (2008b). School-based student support professionals, who are not always mandated in school personnel legislation, tend to be directed toward addressing discrete problems often solved by gate-keeping students into special education services.

When student support professionals are employed by school boards, their services are often underutilized. The promotion of school-family partnerships espoused in educational reform is a task that seldom includes school-based support services professionals. Neither is the task of promoting behavioral discipline through universal programs such as character education and positive behavioral supports. School support services professionals are trained in both mental health and education, which qualifies them to play a major role in addressing barriers to learning.

GOVERNMENT INITIATIVES IN EDUCATION REFORM[2]

Governments have initiated numerous programs to reform publicly funded education. Many of these initiatives, specifically those aimed at closing the achievement gap, should place a greater priority on providing more efficient mental health services in schools through the use of school-based student support services.

As previously stated, the No Child Left Behind Act (NCLB) has put into practice numerous education changes in the United States. NCLB was passed in 2001 and called for comprehensive reforms to reach the national goal of all American students being proficient in reading and mathematics by 2014.

These reforms involve strong assessment and accountability systems, a highly qualified teacher in every classroom, more school choices, an emphasis on school improvement, and using evidence-based teaching practices. However, there is very little in the legislation specifically designed to address mental health issues in children and youth.

Canadian education reform can be illustrated by what the Province of Ontario has put into practice in recent years. The Ministry of Education developed legislation and policies to improve student achievement and reduce the achievement gap while increasing confidence and support for public education. The academic target is to have 75 percent of elementary age children in grades 3 and 6 test at the B level or above by 2010.

Various approaches have been developed to achieve these goals, including large-scale testing, professional learning opportunities for teachers, extra funding for low performing schools, and support of tutoring for underachieving students.

GOVERNMENT INITIATIVES IN
SPECIAL EDUCATION REFORM[3]

Legislation for special education in the United States includes the Individuals with Disabilities Education Act (IDEA), with a precursor first passed in 1975. This legislation is narrowly focused on students with identifiable disabilities that must clearly interfere with educational achievement.

More specifically, students can be identified with emotional problems, (i.e., the category "Emotional Disturbance"); however, the problem must be an identifiable disability, if not diagnosable, and interfere with academic achievement. These students are prescribed related services, such as psychological counseling, functional behavioral assessments, and positive behavioral interventions and supports.

In 2001, less than 1 percent of all students were identified within the category of Emotional Disturbance and received special education or related services under IDEA. These students constituted 8.1 percent of all identified disabilities. This statistic is perplexing, given the fact that approximately 20 percent of children and youth have mental health issues.

NCLB offers an emphasis on evidence-based strategies such as character education, safe school initiatives, and prevention activities. These include programs for students abusing substances, and those suffering from abuse, neglect, or witnessing violence. Both IDEA and NCLB encourage interagency collaboration as a means of enhancing service capacity.

Ontario, as an example of Canadian special education legislation, did not offer special education programs and services until Bill 82 was passed in 1980. Students with special education needs were often placed, for at least part of the school day, in segregated classes. In 1998, Regulation 181/98 deemed that a regular class with appropriate supports should be the first placement considered for exceptional pupils.

Presently, most students with special needs spend at least 50 percent of their day in the regular education classroom. The percentage of students receiving special education composed 12.9 percent of the total student population in 2003–2004. Students identified under the Behavior category totaled 7.3 percent of all identified students.

The percentage of Ontario students receiving special education services who are placed in regular classrooms in 2003–2004 was 81 percent. In addition, the reported incidence of high needs (generally referring to students with intense behaviors who require at least one-on-one supervision) doubled from 2001 to 2004, from 1.4 to 2.8 percent of all students.

Students with mental health issues receive limited supports for their specific needs. In the United States, approximately three-quarters of students who receive mental health services receive it at school from a variety of school-based and non-school-based resources. In fact, some researchers state that the American education system can be considered the de facto mental health system for children in the country.

Many researchers refer to the minimal progress to date in developing effective strategies to improve on school mental health. Some of the challenges these authors discuss include the almost exclusive focus on improving academic achievement. Concomitantly, there is an overreliance on outcome measures of academic achievement and progress, often determined through high-stakes testing. Many proponents of school-based mental health espouse nonacademic outcome measures, such as the development of competencies in social and emotional functioning.

Susan Neuman is the former assistant secretary of Elementary and Secondary Education in the Department of Education in the United States during the G. W. Bush administration. She states that closing the achievement gap requires much more than raising academic standards. She believes that schools in the United States are de facto remedial, clinical institutions, and struggle in the role. She supports a "bolder" educational approach where prevention programs can change the odds for students who come from highly vulnerable and dysfunctional environments (Neuman 2008). A broader and bolder approach that would include school-based mental health services is presented as an efficient method to improve student achievement.

The Canadian Psychological Association presented a position paper that supports broadening the scope of school-based support services (psychologists in particular) as a means of increasing the quality of education. The position paper states that providing timely access to these support services can maximize student potential (2002a). However, school-based psychologists are often not mandated services, and are not included in per pupil funding ratios. They are seldom asked to be part of system planning processes (2002b).

The recommended benchmark for school psychologists is a ratio of 1 psychologist to 1,000 students; however, the reported average ratio across

Canada was 1:5161. A survey conducted by the National Association of School Psychologists in the United States recently found,that the average ratio of school psychologists to students was 1:1621. In addition, of the approximately five hundred thousand social workers in the United States, only 5 percent work in the school system.

There are many recent reports and initiatives developed by various government departments that address students facing barriers to learning. The recommended approach is for school districts to work collaboratively with community organizations. Efficient collaboration must include (1) mandated student support professionals, (2) these professionals must be school-based, and (3) these professionals assume the responsibility for coordinating and managing the collaboration with community professionals.

ALTERNATIVE EDUCATION AND BARRIERS TO LEARNING[4]

Alternative education is often recommended for students facing significant barriers to learning. Alternative education in this context refers to nontraditional teaching and learning methods and does not refer to charter, voucher, alternative, or magnet schools or home schooling.

These programs are often school-based (occasionally off-campus) and are designed to meet the specific academic, behavioral, and social needs of students when traditional educational programs cannot. Alternative education reflects approaches to teaching and learning that may be defined as less "mainstream" and more fitting with the needs of the student at that particular period of his or her school career.

These programs are differentiated from the mainstream by small class size, specially trained teachers, and flexible schedules overlying standard curriculum. The general goal is to keep students in school and help prepare them for postsecondary programs and higher education. Enrollment in such programs may lead to graduating directly from the program or to the reintegration of the student into the regular stream. In either case the student continues to be part of the school community.

Researchers examined alternative education programs in Ohio in the early 2000s. They stated that these programs would be more effective with earlier intervention, such as psychological, psychosocial, and educational assessments for these students at the time of referral to the alternative programs. The researchers also commented that many alternative education programs rely on personnel from community agencies to provide student support services, but the lack of integration with the educational system is often problematic, resulting in a lack of coherence and focus for the individual students and the program in general.

CHILD AND YOUTH MENTAL HEALTH REFORM AND THE ROLE OF SCHOOLS[5]

It is undisputed that there has been an increase in the mental health needs of children and youth. Consequently, child and youth mental health reform efforts have consistently mentioned creating comprehensive and integrated systems of care. The role of schools in these systems often includes universal mental health promotion as part of curriculum and relying on teachers to identify potential mental health problems in individual students.

This approach places disproportionate responsibility on educators. Their roles are academic in nature and we believe that mental health issues should be the responsibility of mental health professionals.

MENTAL HEALTH NEEDS IN CHILDREN AND YOUTH

U.S. statistics reveal that between 15 to 20 percent of children and adolescents have mental illness and emotional disturbance. Between 5 and 9 percent of children can be classified with the diagnosis of a serious emotional disturbance that requires significant mental health supports. Among these children and youth, 70 to 80 percent do not receive treatment or receive inadequate treatment.

Comorbid problems, also called secondary diagnoses, include suicide, homicide, substance abuse, child abuse, teenage pregnancy, school dropout, and juvenile crime, and are consequently increasing.

Canadian statistics reveal that 14 percent of children four to seventeen years have significant mental health problems. Fewer than 25 percent of that group receive treatment.

Recent studies in the United States determined that 51 percent of students receiving special education services due to emotional disturbance dropout of school. They earn lower grades and fail more courses than any other group served by special education.

The data presented above reveal additional risk factors, including an overrepresentation of males, African Americans, and children and youth who live in households with multiple risk factors for poor life outcomes. About one-third live in single-parent households with family income below the

poverty level, and one-fifth live in households where the parent is unemployed and not a high school graduate. Almost half live with a person who
has a disability.

The children and youth in these research studies tend to experience
higher levels of stressors such as poverty, immigration, acculturation, and
exposure to violence and trauma. Despite the high need for mental health
services, these children and youth are often underserviced by community
mental health agencies for reasons of accessibility and stigma. This situation
clearly provides support for broader school-based support services, where
stigma is reduced and services are more easily accessible.

GOVERNMENT REPORTS SUPPORTING MENTAL HEALTH
SERVICES IN SCHOOLS

Government reports supporting child and youth mental health reform have
called for either increasing existing or establishing new mental health services in schools. In the United States, there has been a long-standing call for
school-based mental health services. The U.S. Surgeon General's Report
on Mental Health directly referred to mental health barriers to academic
achievement and the importance of school-based mental health services.
The report stated that mental health is essential to social and emotional
development as well as learning (1999).

The report of the President's New Freedom Commission on Mental
Health stated that good mental health is vital for learning. The report supports improving and expanding school mental health programs, because
these programs clearly demonstrate reduced absences and discipline referrals
as well as increased test scores (2003).

Senators Kirby and Keon of the Canadian Standing Committee on
Social Affairs, Science and Technology, authored a report in 2006 entitled
*Out of the Shadows at Last: Transforming Mental Health, Mental Illness and
Addiction Services in Canada.* They made numerous recommendations that
support mental health services in schools.

This report describes the steps involved in developing schools as sites
for effective delivery of mental health services for children and youth. School
boards must mandate the establishment of school-based teams to assist parents
in accessing and navigating mental health services. Some services should be
relocated from hospital or community sites. Teachers should be provided
with the time and resources to take on the new role of early identification so
they can properly refer students to the school teams (Kirby & Keon 2006).

School-based mental health services in these reports refer to variations of collaborative partnerships between community-based mental health services and school employees, most often teachers. These reports leave out what we believe to be an essential component in efficiently servicing students facing mental health issues, namely, school-based support service professionals.

MENTAL HEALTH SERVICES IN SCHOOLS

It has been stated that schools are primarily education institutions and they should not be in the "mental health business." This view is too simplistic. Most students cannot leave their mental health challenges behind when they enter the classroom door. As far back as 1989, the Carnegie Council on Adolescent Development Task Force on the Education of Young Adolescents stated that although schools cannot and should not be held responsible for meeting every need of every student, it is vitally important that schools meet nonacademic challenges that directly affect school success and learning (Carnegie Council 1989).

Where student support mental health services exist, the professionals providing these services are often seen by administrators and educators as "add-ons" or "guests" of the system. This may be due to the perceived incompatibility between the academic interests of educators and the non-academic interests of mental health professionals. This situation often results in an uneasy coordination of programs and services.

Research has clearly shown that programs that increase prosocial behaviors are predictive of performance on standardized academic measures, as well as intellectual functioning. Conversely, antisocial behavior is often linked with poor academic outcomes. Schools are very much aware of these connections, and have long endeavored to address it with a variety of programs. However, these programs are often delivered through collaborative partnerships with community organizations. These programs are apt to be fragmented, too general and not school specific. In addition, accountability can also be an issue.

In the United States, the Department of Health and Human Services implemented a number of initiatives to promote a seamless, community-based system of care that would cover the range of services required for children with mental health problems and their families. The initiatives included variations of formal interagency agreements, blended funding mechanisms, shared personnel, and resource leveraging.

School systems are seen as critical in these partnerships. For example, school-based mental health services provide nonstigmatizing, natural, and easy access. Providing mental health services in schools also facilitates a three-tiered approach of prevention and screening, targeted approaches for at-risk populations, and intensive indicated services for those children and youth with serious emotional and behavioral difficulties.

School-based mental health programs have been shown to have better outcomes than traditional outpatient or residential services. These outcomes include reduced symptoms, decreased school absenteeism and dropout, as well as improved family functioning. In addition there is reduced utilization of more intense or restrictive services including mental health and residential services.

EVIDENCE-BASED SCHOOL MENTAL HEALTH INTERVENTIONS

There is growing research on evidence-based school mental health interventions. Although the research is limited, there is ample evidence to indicate that such interventions are regarded as some of the most efficient and effective ways to deal with mental health issues in schools.

School-based interventions are seen as

- Improving limited access to mental health services for children and youth
- Reducing the effects of stigma
- Representing a single location through which a majority of children and youth with mental health issues can be reached
- Providing an optimal environment for prevention services
- Providing early identification and intervention efforts that prevent the development of secondary dysfunction such as substance abuse and suicidal behaviors

Ease of access for children and families is a critical determinant in success of treatment for mental health issues. "No show" rates of over 50 percent are common in community-based practices. Researchers list a number of reasons why 40 to 60 percent of families prematurely terminate their involvement with community-based treatment organizations. They are reluctant to utilize community-based mental health services, because of access issues (time, distance), stigma, frustration due to disconnected services, and in certain areas, high costs. Many of these issues are not a concern if treatment occurs in the school setting. We would add lack of familiarity with community agencies and long waiting lists as additional factors that can discourage families from initiating contact in the first place.

There are several research centers in the United States that investigate, support, and advocate for school-based mental health (SBMH) services, notably the UCLA Center for Mental Health in Schools and the Center for School Mental Health Analysis and Action at the University of Maryland. These are federally funded programs created to support the integration of mental health services in schools and broader instructional reforms.

Other research centers include the Research and Training Center for Children's Mental Health at the University of South Florida, the Center for School-based Mental Health Programs at Miami University, Ohio, and the Center for the Advancement of Mental Health Practices in Schools in Missouri. Their research has shown that evidence-based school mental health interventions can have a positive impact on many areas of psychological and academic functioning.

There is research evidence that supports the advantages of providing mental health services by school-based professionals. Although not the initial intention of their research, Crisp and colleagues found that the provision of evidence-based treatment in schools ran more smoothly when practitioners were already employed by the schools. This finding was due to the fact that the school-based professionals were better connected with both the students and school staff (2006).

Massey and colleagues compared school-based versus community-based service providers of both prevention and intervention programs in schools. These programs included prevention services, such as antiviolence, social skills, and leadership training. Intervention services included anger management, parent advocacy, alternatives to suspensions, and family therapy (2005).

After the services were delivered, both the school and community-based providers were interviewed in focus groups. Findings revealed that utilizing school-based professionals resulted in fewer problems with accessibility and acceptance of both prevention and intervention programs. These programs were more sustainable, there was less teacher resistance, and program development and coordination was more straightforward.

The authors also stated that school-based professionals have a knowledge base in both education and mental health. They are able to integrate mental health services into schools and provide prevention programs as part of the broader curriculum to address barriers to learning. These professionals can contribute to the collaboration process in a unique manner, utilizing their problem-solving expertise, their mental health knowledge, and their familiarity with the school culture (Massey et al. 2005).

Additional research has shown that families become more involved in school-based mental health services than clinic-based services. School-based mental health services have also been shown to add the following positive outcomes:

- Improved achievement
- Improved attendance
- Improvements in school climates
- Reduced reliance on referrals to special education
- Reduced reliance on school suspensions as a discipline method

In Baltimore schools, over 95 percent of students referred to and seen four or more times by school-based mental health clinicians did not receive any more suspensions.

As research has shown, school-based mental health professionals provide a unique perspective that enables them to effectively bridge the mental health and academic sectors for students facing barriers to learning.

IDEAS TO CONSIDER

- Education reforms normally recommend closing the achievement gap through improvements in school leadership and pedagogy.
- Education reform acknowledges mental health problems in students; however, reforms suggest interventions generally be carried out by community-based services in or out of schools.
- Child and youth mental health reform mentions schools, but does so in a limited context with a narrow focus.
- Child and youth mental health reform suggests that teachers take on two additional roles: (1) early identifiers of student mental health problems, and (2) providers of mental health promotion and prevention programs.
- Many integrated school mental health programs do not consistently or fully utilize school-based student support services professionals.
- Research has shown the advantages of having school-based student support services professionals provide mental health services for children and youth.
- School-based student support professionals, who are trained in both education and mental health, should play a key role in school mental health.

6

SCHOOL SYSTEM APPROACHES
TO BARRIERS TO LEARNING

A ll school systems recognize that barriers to learning exist and that these barriers need to be addressed in order to improve student achievement. The extent to which mental health issues in students are considered varies. Consequently, there are variations among school systems with respect to intervention for students facing barriers to learning. These variations are discussed in detail below.

THE BASIC MODEL

Figure 6.1 represents a basic model of practice that school systems utilize to address barriers to learning. The upper left circle represents Administration, which includes activities conducted by senior management such as directors and superintendents, and site management such as school principals and vice principals. The upper right circle represents Instruction, which includes activities conducted by coordinators, consultants, classroom teachers, and resource teachers.

The lower circle represents activities addressing barriers to learning, both academic and nonacademic. These activities can include reducing, preventing, and managing barriers to learning. The upper portion where the circles cross represents the activities conducted by both administration and instruction. The bottom of the lower circle refers to any activities that are specifically planned to reduce barriers to learning by noneducators. Students and their families as well as classrooms are represented by the area where the circles intersect.

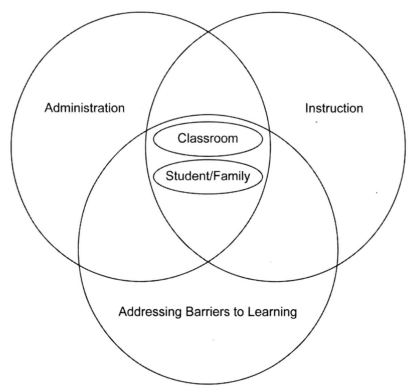

Figure 6.1. School System Approach to Address Barriers to Learning: The Basic Model

Below we discuss variations of the basic model that we believe represent school system approaches to addressing barriers to learning. The differences between the approaches lie in (1) the degree to which the school system believes that high-quality leadership and instruction are all that is necessary to reduce *all* barriers, (2) the degree to which the school system acknowledges the use of support services professionals to address these barriers, and (3) whether these professionals should be community-based, school-based, or a combination of the two.

We illustrate these different approaches by adjusting the size of the Administration, Instruction, and Addressing Barriers to Learning circles. We caution the reader to keep in mind that the circles represent activities, particularly methods to address barriers to learning. When the circles are reduced in size, it merely reflects less involvement in addressing barriers to learning, not less involvement in leadership or instruction.

ADMINISTRATION AND INSTRUCTION

Figure 6.2 represents school systems that endorse the concept that improved and effective leadership and teaching alone will successfully address all barriers to learning, both academic and nonacademic. In these systems, barriers to learning, whether they be student- or classroom-based, are addressed primarily by the efforts of school leadership and teachers. These systems do not utilize the services of multidisciplinary student support services professionals to assist in addressing barriers to learning.

The unshaded part of the lower circle represents barriers that are not addressed. We believe there are few systems that currently utilize this approach. Most advocates of education reform promote formal and informal partnerships with community organizations as a means of addressing nonacademic barriers to learning.

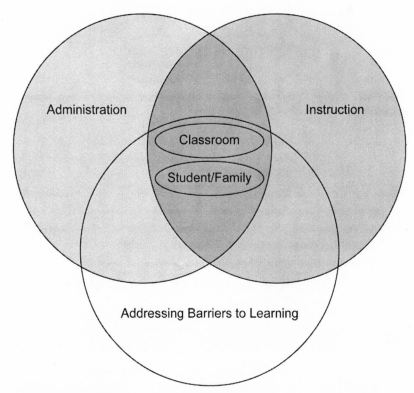

Figure 6.2. School System Approach to Address Barriers to Learning: Administration and Instruction

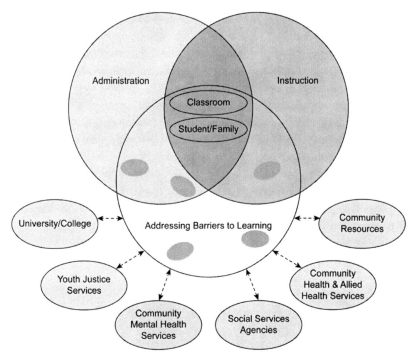

Figure 6.3. School System Approach to Address Barriers to Learning: Informal Partnerships with Community Organizations

INFORMAL PARTNERSHIPS WITH COMMUNITY ORGANIZATIONS

Figure 6.3 represents school systems that acknowledge that administration and instruction alone cannot address *all* barriers to learning. The leadership and instruction circles are smaller than in figure 6.2, representing less involvement in addressing barriers to learning.

These school systems address certain barriers to learning, particularly nonacademic ones, through referrals to community organizations. This is accomplished by establishing partnerships with community-based organizations that are represented by the ovals in the bottom part of figure 6.3. The organizations are described below.

COMMUNITY MENTAL HEALTH AND ADDICTION SERVICES

These organizations are often the most frequent resources used to address nonacademic barriers to learning, such as individual treatment, medication management, group counseling, and family therapy. These services would be provided by child and family mental health clinics, hospital inpatient and outpatient units, treatment centers, addiction services, and private mental health practitioners.

SOCIAL SERVICES AGENCIES

These agencies are, in our opinion, the next most frequently utilized resource. They include, but are not limited to, child protection services, welfare services, housing services, and victim services. Supports include child, youth, and family counseling, as well as crisis intervention in abuse or severe behavior situations, economic support for families living in poverty, and shelter for families involved in domestic abuse.

COMMUNITY HEALTH AND ALLIED HEALTH SERVICES

These organizations include hospital inpatient and outpatient services, clinics, and private practitioners. Public health services would also be included here. Activities would include medication follow-up, and individual and group treatment interventions.

Youth Justice Services

These services include police, probation, courts, corrections, and alternative justice services. An example of partnerships with youth justice services is when police officers are assigned as "school resource officers," regularly providing prevention and intervention services to a number of schools in a specific geographic area.

LOCAL ORGANIZATIONS

These organizations include service and volunteer organizations, faith-based organizations, cultural institutions, and business and professional organizations. Examples of activities could include sponsoring school breakfast clubs, sports programs, leadership training, and arts instruction.

UNIVERSITIES/COLLEGES

Institutions of higher learning are not used by school systems in a direct referral manner. These institutions provide training for professionals who

work in some school systems and all the other organizations mentioned above, often referred to in the literature as "preservice." In school systems, universities and colleges often provide interns who spend some time training in school systems. Colleges and universities utilize the resources of school systems to provide a supply of subjects for their research activities, but may at times provide different interventions to reduce or prevent barriers to learning.

EXAMPLES OF PROFESSIONALS PRACTICING IN COMMUNITY ORGANIZATIONS

Child and youth workers
Counselors
Family physicians
Graduate students in mental health postsecondary programs
Nurses
Nurse practitioners
Occupational therapists
Pediatricians
Pastoral counselors
Physical therapists
Police officers
Probation officers
Professors and other postsecondary instructors/supervisors
Psychiatrists
Psychologists
Social workers
Speech-language pathologists

In this school system approach, students and families are directed by school personnel to seek assistance outside of the school system. Sometimes, these partnerships involve outside organizations treating students in the school building. More often, students and families who are receiving treatment do so at the organization's premises in the community.

The connections that are made between schools and community-based organizations in figure 6.3 are mostly informal; students and their families are encouraged by school personnel to access the community-based services where available. These recommendations may require referrals from family doctors or direct parent or youth initiation.

Addressing barriers to learning through this approach is often inefficient and ineffective. We represent this inefficiency through the broken lines that partially link the community-based organizations with the school system. Even though the arrows go both ways, the community organizations determine the nature and duration of the intervention.

The shaded small ovals within the lower circle represent how the school system, with input from the community organizations, addresses barriers to learning. The shaded parts are scattered, fragmented, and not connected with each other, representing an inefficient and incomplete approach to addressing barriers to learning.

SCHOOL-BASED MULTIDISCIPLINARY SUPPORT SERVICES TEAMS AND COMMUNITY ORGANIZATIONS

Figure 6.4 represents what we believe are the majority of school systems in large urban areas. The arrows connecting the community-based organizations

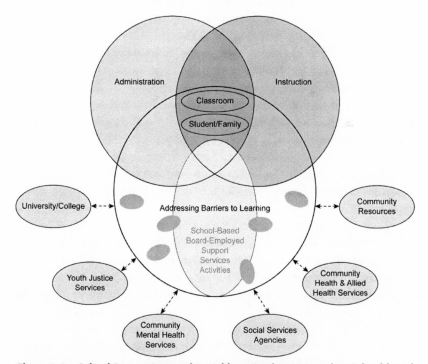

Figure 6.4. School System Approach to Address Barriers to Learning: School-based Student Support Services Teams and Community Organizations

with the school system are broken because they still fall short of completely addressing barriers to learning. In this figure, we introduce school-based board-employed support service activities. This is represented by the large oval contained within the lower circle.

The small shaded ovals within the lower circle represent community-based organizations working with school-based professionals to address barriers to learning. The small ovals are scattered and haphazardly distributed, and only some of them are connected with the large oval representing school-based support service activities. There are still white areas in the lower circle, indicating that many barriers are not fully addressed.

LIMITATIONS OF SCHOOL SYSTEM METHODS FOR ADDRESSING BARRIERS TO LEARNING[1]

Community-based organizations that deal with child and youth mental health have often been characterized in the literature as fragmented and having little connection with each other. Community organizations tend to connect with school boards independently and in a fragmented manner that is not always in the best interests of the school system.

Community organizations service the community. When their services are contracted by school systems, it is important to realize that schools are not their only clients. Outcome measures differ widely in terms of successful intervention. Many community-based services use reduction of symptoms as outcome measures, while school-based services measure outcome by increased academic achievement as well as symptom reduction.

Community-based services are often selective in their client base. There are many criteria required to access community-based services. Some examples of these criteria: referrals must originate from physicians, clients must reside in a particular catchment area, clients with specific or multiple diagnoses are excluded, and parents must make a commitment to be part of the treatment. Due to the fact that all children and youth are in school, these criteria do not apply for school-based support services when students are referred. Student support services are expected to accept all referrals.

Treatment in community-based organizations sometimes cannot be accessed until the student's problems are severe or have reached a crisis situation. Community-based services can also at times close cases for a variety of reasons, such as clients missing a number of consecutive appointments.

In some cases, both community- and school-based student support personnel work with the same student at the same time, and may not be aware of each other's involvement. In particular, school-based support services are seldom notified by the community organization. On occasion, when both professionals are aware of each other's involvement with a student, the community organization's psychologist will assess the student's emotional and behavioral functioning. Then, the community organizations may request that the school psychologist only assess a student's academic and intellectual functioning. Such a fragmented approach not only duplicates services, but leaves the results of the assessment open to question.

Full-service community schools are an example of community-based services carried out on school premises. These school-linked partnerships are popular in the United States as they provide health services in areas where the majority of people are uninsured for health services. The goals are to access additional resources and reduce nonteaching demands on school staff.

These full-service community schools are also intended to provide opportunities to enhance students' emotional, social, and physical development. Most often, local child and youth mental health centers have staff come into the schools regularly to meet with families encountering problems.

Additional research has demonstrated that although full-service community schools can produce some gains in achievement, they are not designed to address all barriers to learning. Only 60 percent of these school-based health centers provide mental health services. Moreover, there is little, if any, integration with existing school-based support services professionals and the services they are already providing.

Research that reviewed school mental health services found that only 50 percent of American middle and high schools offered mental health intervention. The majority of schools in the review did not employ or provide specialty mental health professionals, or did so infrequently. Services mostly consisted of evaluation and referral to community services. It was not always clear in the research if the services were provided on-site or linked with community-based services. There was limited evidence that such referrals were effective in providing access to community-based mental health services.

The mental health services that were reviewed in this research were not clearly defined and covered everything from crisis counseling to psychological testing. It was reported that 80 percent of school mental health services provided evaluation of emotional and behavior problems (not treatment) and 56 percent provided counseling. Of these schools, 41 percent contracted or employed psychologists, 21 percent employed social workers, and 2.1 percent employed psychiatrists. Not surprisingly, urban, suburban, and large schools were more likely to have mental health services than rural and small schools.

POPULATION-BASED APPROACHES TO
ADDRESSING BARRIERS TO LEARNING[2]

Proponents of evidence-based school-based mental health services support a population-based approach to addressing barriers to learning. The University of South Florida Research and Training Center for Children's Mental Health used a public health system approach to develop a four-step system that addresses *all* students' mental health needs, including mental health promotion, prevention, early intervention, and treatment of severe challenges (Kutash, Duchnowski, & Lynn 2006).

The first step in a population-based approach involves a systematic needs assessment in the community or school. The second step is identifying students' current risk and protective factors. The third and fourth steps involve implementing carefully chosen interventions and evaluating and monitoring their effectiveness and impact. Other researchers have added steps to implementing a population-based approach for school-based mental health services, such as diagnostic, research, and training components.

Population-based approaches are often illustrated with a triangle, representing three basic tiers of intervention: universal, targeted, and indicated. Figure 6.5 illustrates the triangle and the level of needs and interventions for a population. Before providing population-based services, a needs assessment is conducted by screening the entire population. The results of this screening measure provide information on who needs which level of intervention.

There are two methods of providing these services. The first method is to place individuals in specific levels of intervention as a result of their scores on the basic screening measure. The second method, often referred to as response to intervention, is to start every individual at the universal level and move them up to the next level if they are not able to benefit from the previous intervention level. Additional measures of response are often conducted to determine if individuals are benefitting from intervention at their present level.

There are three tiers of intervention. The bottom of the triangle represents Universal Interventions, for all of the particular population being served. Generally, these interventions are all that is required for about 80 to 90 percent of the population. The individuals who do not benefit from universal intervention are represented in the upper two levels of the triangle.

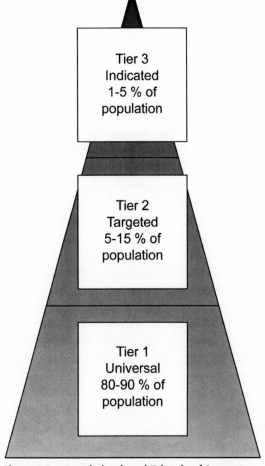

Figure 6.5.   Population-based Triangle of Supports

The middle of the triangle represents Targeted Interventions, which refers to services for a select group who do not benefit from universal interventions. These individuals are deemed to be at risk for more serious problems. The idea is to provide early intervention to prevent the problem from becoming more severe. Approximately 5 to 15 percent of the population benefit from these targeted services.

Approximately 1 to 5 percent of the population do not benefit from targeted services. The top third of the triangle, Indicated Interventions, refers to services for this portion of the population. Their problems are severe and require intense intervention.

COMMON APPROACH TO ADDRESSING
BARRIERS TO LEARNING: THE INVERTED TRIANGLE[3]

A population-based approach can reduce costs when providing services for students facing barriers to learning. This approach avoids higher monetary and resource costs compared to waiting until problems require intense services. Otherwise, problems can become chronic and intractable, contributing to ever-growing waiting lists. Research has shown that prevention, specifically population-based services in schools performed by school-based support services staff, can eliminate long waiting lists for assessments.

As seen in figure 6.3, some school systems rely on outside organizations to provide specific intense interventions for the few students who exhibit severe challenges. We can contrast this with systems, as seen in figure 6.4, where services are provided by both school-based support services professionals and community organizations. However, both systems spend much of their time servicing individual students facing severe challenges. In these systems, there are few population-based services that can provide prevention as an intervention.

In figure 6.6, we employ the population-based approach triangle and invert it to represent schools systems that do not employ a population-based approach. In these cases, school-based support services professionals spend the majority of their time supporting individual students with high needs. If these students are receiving intervention from community organizations, there is often little integration with the school system.

On the left of the figure, we represent the number of students serviced, the severity of their behavioral needs, and the relative risk they have of presenting challenges in school. In the center of the figure, we use population-based services terminology to categorize the support the students require, as well as an estimate of the amount of time school support services personnel spend with these students. On the right of the figure, we give examples of support and management activities provided by school-based support services professionals.

The bottom tier of the triangle represents universal interventions. These services are for all students from low to high levels of risk for challenges. We estimate that school-based support service professionals spend approximately 1 to 5 percent of their time on universal interventions. This low number is directly related to limited school-based resources and time. These interventions may consist of prevention programs and mental health education. Examples would include schoolwide positive behavior supports, character education, and antibullying programs.

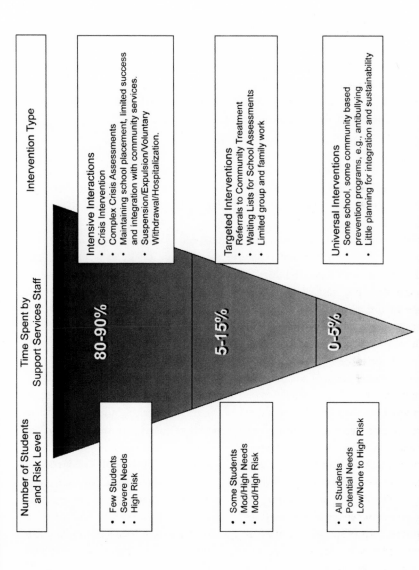

Figure 6.6. Common Approach to Address Barriers to Learning: The Inverted Triangle

Number of Students and Risk Level

Time Spent by Support Services Staff

Intervention Type

80-90%

5-15%

0-5%

Intensive Interactions
- Crisis Intervention
- Complex Crisis Assessments
- Maintaining school placement, limited success and integration with community services.
- Suspension/Expulsion/Voluntary Withdrawal/Hospitalization.

Targeted Interventions
- Referrals to Community Treatment
- Waiting Lists for School Assessments
- Limited group and family work

Universal Interventions
- Some school, some community based prevention programs, e.g., antibullying
- Little planning for integration and sustainability

- Few Students
- Severe Needs
- High Risk

- Some Students
- Mod/High Needs
- Mod/High Risk

- All Students
- Potential Needs
- Low/None to High Risk

The middle tier of the triangle represents targeted interventions. We estimate that approximately 5 to 15 percent of school-based support services professionals' time is spent with students at risk for challenging behaviors. These students have been identified as having problems and their needs are deemed as moderate to high. Some of these school-based interventions may include assessments and family involvement, but due to limitations in time and resources, can involve referrals to community treatment.

The uppermost tier of the triangle represents intensive intervention. We estimate that approximately 80 to 90 percent of school-based support services professionals spend their time in intensive interventions. This work is done individually or in small groups of students.

ADVANTAGES OF SCHOOL-BASED SUPPORT SERVICES IMPLEMENTING A POPULATION-BASED APPROACH TO ADDRESS BARRIERS TO LEARNING[4]

The Center for Mental Health in Schools calls for moving toward population-based approaches and reducing the reliance on person-centered pathology in the schools (2008a). It therefore seems logical to move toward integrating population-based mental health services for children and youth within the school system. Presently, the majority of child and youth mental health services commonly consists of specific programs, often developed through university research, that are provided at children's mental health centers or some type of community-based practice.

Schools are able to span the entire continuum of service need, that is, all three tiers of a population-based approach. Instead of waiting for referrals of students who are already experiencing mental health difficulties, schools are able to easily provide universal preventive interventions that promote mental health and social adjustment.

Heathfield and Clark are two researchers in school-based mental health who state that schools provide the most suitable site for case management, even at the intensive level. These researchers specifically suggest that case managers be school-based mental health professionals who provide intensive monitoring and intervention (2004). Professionals in this role can ensure that the delivery of services is integrated and meets the changing needs of students and their families.

Despite the advantages of school-based support professionals providing population-based approaches, many jurisdictions do not have policies that can support this practice. It is our opinion that school-based support service professionals will not be able to support all three levels of a population-based approach without mandates requiring their involvement at all levels, including case management.

RESEARCH ON POPULATION-BASED APPROACHES TO ADDRESSING BARRIERS TO LEARNING[5]

Canadian researchers in an Ontario study consulted with frontline school support service professionals (DeBeer & Gairey 2008). A number of principles for best practices were developed. These principles are summarized below.

- Student support services are essential to student well-being.
- These services should be provided by school board–employed professionals and available to all students on an annualized basis, with dedicated, predictable, stable, and sufficient funding.
- The nonacademic needs of students within the school system must be met by school-based support services professionals.
- The practice model needs to include prevention, consultation, intervention, and assessment within a multidisciplinary collaborative and flexible team.
- This team plays a central role in liaison with the community, school board, school, class, and student.
- School-based support professionals need to be involved in planning protocols and procedures at the school board level, especially those provided by community organizations.

This research also identified difficulties inherent in currently popular government-sponsored collaborative projects. Community organizations, even when in partnership with school boards, tend to offer services based on their own models and not on students' needs. Furthermore, targeted initiatives and specific projects may raise false expectations when sustainability is compromised by such factors as one-time funding. Both administrators and school-based support services professionals, not surprisingly, identified that the preferred model would involve services delivered directly in the school.

In the United States, there are a number of university research centers investigating, studying, and promoting school mental health. Many of these programs rely on school-linked approaches where university researchers or community organizations partner with school academic staff to deliver services to students. Surprisingly, few utilize school-based support services professionals, considering the advantages of this approach shown in the research discussed in chapter 5.

The Center for Mental Health in Schools at UCLA (smhp.psych.ucla.edu) works to improve outcomes for students by providing a comprehensive website. This site offers resources, technical assistance, and leadership training institutes, as well as networking opportunities.

The Collaborative for Academic, Social, and Emotional Learning supports universal educational programs for promoting positive social and emotional skills such as self-awareness, self-management, responsible decision making, and resiliency (www.casel.org). Some jurisdictions in the United States, such as Iowa and Illinois, have social-emotional learning initiatives mandated into curriculum.

The Center for School Mental Health at the University of Maryland in Baltimore (csmh.umaryland.edu) provides services to strengthen policies and programs in school mental health to improve learning and promote child and youth success. They support the development of a broad and growing community of practice through a companion website called the School Mental Health Connection (www.schoolmentalhealth.org). This site develops and presents resources to introduce and enhance mental health services in schools.

The Center for School-based Mental Health Programs at Miami University in Ohio (www.units.muohio.edu/csbmhp) is building collaborative relationships with schools and community organizations to address mental health and school success in students. Their objective is to advance this agenda through applied research, preservice and in-service training of education and mental health professionals, as well as direct service.

The Center for the Advancement of Mental Health Practices in Schools provides resources, professional development training, as well as a unique graduate degree in mental health in schools (education.missouri.edu/orgs/camhps/).

The University of South Florida's Research and Training Center for Children's Mental Health (rtckids.fmhi.usf.edu) researches the foundations for effective systems of care and works to improve services for children and families with serious emotional or behavioral disorders, achieved through research, training, consultation, and dissemination activities. This center also advocates for a population-based approach to addressing barriers to learning and improved outcomes for children and youth with mental health issues.

The Positive Behavioral Interventions and Supports website (www.pbis.org) provides resources and tools to implement schoolwide universal programs in behavioral support and discipline that enhances students' social development and learning.

The Center for School Mental Health at the University of Maryland in Baltimore, together with the IDEA Partnership, have created a website (www.sharedwork.org) to house communities of practice that work together to advance, among other educational topics, school-based mental health.

The Canadian School Health Knowledge Network supports a community of practice in school mental health. Their website offers information on coordinated strategies for mental health in schools (shtoolbox -mentalhealth.wetpaint.com). These strategies include the following programs: stigma reduction through classroom instruction, youth engagement activities, parent involvement, mental health services, and policy revisions for school discipline and other interventions. The website offers discussion groups for school-community organization partnerships.

One research study surveyed over four hundred stakeholders in mental health, education, school mental health, and family members. These stakeholders rated population-based school mental health programs high in satisfaction and to be contributing to outcomes valued by families and schools alike (Weist et al. 2005).

The researchers noted that several program requirements were necessary to achieve positive outcomes. Teachers, students, and their families need to be actively involved in all program elements, including development, governance, and evaluation. In addition, programs must be based on a continuum of interventions.

Family and youth representation is essential when providing programs to address barriers to learning. When mental health promotion and intervention involves adolescents, it is important to include them as partners in planning and implementation. The unique needs and concerns of each family, within the context of cultural, socioeconomic, and religious differences are paramount. It is important to involve families at all levels of programming for services for their children.

Supporting families in their children's education has been shown to have positive outcomes with respect to learning. This concept is also discussed in the education reform literature. Family involvement is important in today's increasingly diverse school populations. Support services need to be culturally competent, and training of all stakeholders in diversity issues is paramount.

School-based student support services should be mandated and broadened in order to effectively integrate the two systems. These professionals can be instrumental in providing a seamless delivery of services to ensure the best outcome for children and youth facing barriers to learning.

IDEAS TO CONSIDER

- Barriers to learning exist and need to be addressed in order to improve student achievement.
- Variations exist in how school systems address mental health issues in students.
- School systems can utilize a population-based approach for addressing all barriers to learning, including the three tiers of intervention: universal, targeted, and indicated.
- Some school systems utilize their school-based support services professionals only at the indicated intervention level.
- School systems should begin to utilize school-based support services professionals in all three tiers of population-based interventions to address barriers to learning.

7

REDUCTION, MANAGEMENT, AND PREVENTION OF BARRIERS TO LEARNING

The School-based Integrated Support Services Model (SISSM)

Current literature and numerous reports on closing the achievement gap and addressing child and youth mental health issues support locating more mental health programs in schools through partnerships. This colocation of services is often referred to as integration. Although locating mental health services in schools would provide community-based mental health professionals easier access to their clients, we feel that the issue is more complex than accessibility of service location; there are four principle reasons why this situation is complex.

Firstly, many partnerships between school systems and community organizations that address barriers to learning are unstructured and lack sustainability. Such partnerships are limited and often consist of simply colocating services in school, or are based on one-time projects. These services can function in isolation with respect to any similar nonacademic support services already occurring in the schools. Goals of such services may be actually competing with academic and student support services goals.

Secondly, colocation of services in schools often present difficulties because of differing interests between the community organizations and schools. These differences are commonly referred to as "silos." The existence of silos has often been discussed as a contributor to difficulties in successful partnerships. This is due to the fact that the partnership organizations may not have a complete understanding of each other's procedures, training, cultures, and even areas of expertise.

Thirdly, in some partnerships, professionals in both schools and community organizations may feel that their own employment is at risk, compromising any planned collaboration. As well, liability, informed consent, and confidentiality issues are often not adequately addressed.

Fourthly, partnerships are at times focused on individual pathologies such as discrete diagnoses. Services can consist of individual interventions for students with the highest needs. With this approach, long wait lists for service will persist. Services seldom take into account all aspects of a three-tiered population-based approach. Prevention, early identification, and intervention services are a reasonable way of reducing waiting lists for high-needs individual services.

In order to address the problems with partnerships expressed above, we believe that integrated services require the perspective of school-based support services professionals. This would be accomplished by providing a core group of school-based support services professionals in each school. School-based support services professionals are the most appropriate personnel to bridge the systems and cultures of education and mental health. These professionals have knowledge of both education and clinical services.

This core group of school-based professionals would manage the school-linked services of other community organizations when the services are addressing barriers to learning. We propose a model that can facilitate the implementation of these services, the School-based Integrated Support Services Model (SISSM).

We believe SISSM can address academic and nonacademic barriers to learning with greater effectiveness and efficiency than the other models we have previously discussed (see chapter 6). SISSM targets all three tiers of a population-based approach (universal, targeted, and indicated) as a means of addressing *all* barriers to learning. This model includes addressing students influenced by the Multi-Ripple Effect, a group whose needs have been largely overlooked.

SISSM involves the following interventions:

- Full population-based continuum of services
  - Mental health promotion
  - Prevention
  - Early intervention
  - Treatment
  - Chronic care
- Fully integrated evidence-based services for children and youth
- Exceptional school leadership and instruction with appropriate numbers of professional school-based support service professionals and community organization staffing established through locally determined needs and resources
- Continuous intake through a three-tiered approach

IMPLEMENTATION OF POPULATION-BASED
SERVICES TO ADDRESS BARRIERS TO LEARNING: SISSM[1]

There are different approaches to implementing a population-based system to address barriers to learning. One is a top-down approach, where the initial decision to implement and manage a population-based approach to address barriers to learning is made at a top administrative level. The other is a bottom-up approach, more of a grassroots method where pilot projects are introduced, often at an individual school level. The projects expand through their success. For example, school psychologists can implement a targeted intervention program for students showing early signs of anxiety.

Our recommended approach to servicing children and youth in schools is represented in figure 7.1. This is the final representation of the

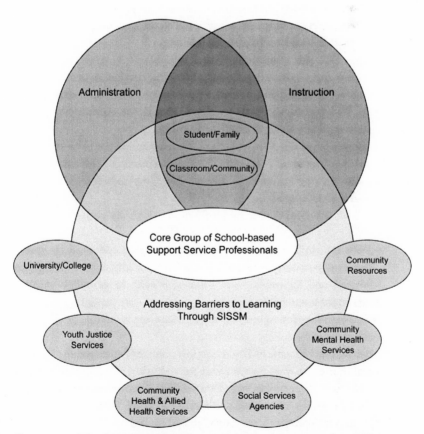

Figure 7.1. School System Approach to Address Barriers to Learning: SISSM

basic model introduced in chapter 6 (figures 6.1, 6.2, 6.3, and 6.4) representing school system responses to addressing barriers to learning.

In figure 7.1, the Addressing Barriers to Learning circle is larger than in the previous figures. As well, this circle is larger than the Administration and Instruction circles in the previous figures. This represents a decrease in Administration and Instructional involvement with respect to addressing nonacademic barriers to learning. The lower circle is bigger than in previous figures, indicating increased involvement from the support services professionals. Also, the lower circle is completely shaded in, indicating that the barriers to learning are completely addressed. These barriers are managed, reduced, or prevented through universal, targeted, and indicated interventions.

The white oval integrated into all circles in the center of the Venn diagram represents a core group of school-based support services professionals. One or more of these professionals are assigned to each school to ensure that services provided by community organizations are integrated in order to effectively address barriers to learning.

Notice that the community-based organizations' ovals are partially placed within the circle representing addressing barriers to learning. Part of the ovals representing community organizations' services remain outside the circle. This represents professional activities in the community that do not concern students facing barriers to learning.

In the center of the Venn diagram, we have added the term *community* in addition to "students," "families," and "classrooms." This addition reflects the fact that the community is better integrated into the interventions addressing barriers to learning.

SISSM is accomplished through the following measures:

- Both school and community organizations would need to ensure that the professionals would have training in implementing a population-based approach. This training would be provided through in-service for existing personnel. Support for changing preservice training to include population-based services would be provided by the university/college organizations.
- An increase in school-based support services professionals, through reallocation, redeployment, and restructuring of school- and community-based services based on locally determined needs and resources would be needed (see level 4 of figure 7.2).
- When community-based professionals are redeployed or reallocated to school-linked services, they will likely already have sufficient train-

ing in child and youth mental health. However, they will require specific training in school culture and issues affecting learning.

- A core group of school-based support services professionals at the local school level coordinates community-based organizations servicing the school population.
- The core group would require specific training in mental health and education, as well as managerial skills.
- The additional school-based support services professionals are now able to utilize a population-based approach where universal, targeted, and indicated interventions for barriers to learning are implemented. This model should provide additional professional

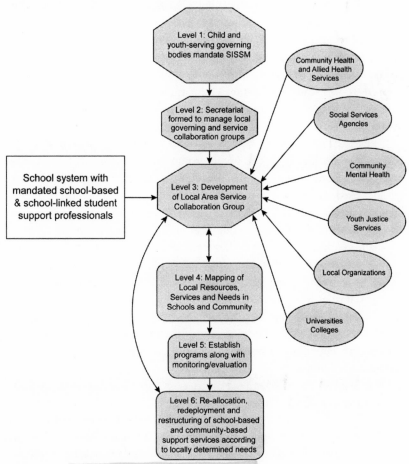

Figure 7.2. Proposed Implementation of SISSM

resources to ensure a full continuum of services from mental health promotion to chronic care.

Figure 7.2 represents the progression of steps that leads to implementation of SISSM. We advocate for a mixed top-down/bottom-up approach. In level 1, child- and youth-serving governing bodies (i.e., government departments such as education and child services) mandate the implementation of a school-based integrated support services model. We believe that mandating SISSM, the top-down portion of the approach, is required to initiate a population-based approach to addressing barriers to learning. Preliminary funding to facilitate the changes to an integrated population-based service model may be necessary in some jurisdictions.

Level 2 denotes the development of an upper level of governance or overarching body. This would be a secretariat with dedicated staff whose responsibility is to manage the remaining levels of the model's implementation, as well as managing any required preliminary funding to support changes in system delivery. At this level, systemwide guidance and leadership create the readiness for the systematic change to implement SISSM. This entity will ensure the coordination and integration of services with instructional and educational leadership components.

Level 3 comprises the development of multiple service collaboration groups that are locally based. These groups would consist of leaders from both the school system on the left side (educators, administrators, and school-based student support services) and the community organizations depicted on the right side of figure 7.2. Parent and youth representatives are also included in the process. Education and multidisciplinary professional associations and unions, where they exist, should be involved.

We recommend that the chairperson of each service collaboration group be a school-based student support professional who already has a managerial role. It is important that the chairperson has a working knowledge of both schools and community organizations. This local group will meet regularly, but may rotate meeting locations to different schools and community organization premises to promote a better understanding of each other's cultures, norms, and practices.

In level 4, the service collaboration group performs a comprehensive mapping activity. This activity consists of enumerating existing local resources, services, and programs, performing a gap analysis, surveying unmet needs, and identifying desired outcomes. Here is where nonproductive services, duplication of services, and fragmentation will be identified. Existing programs need to be catalogued as to which tier they represent.

At the beginning of the process, it is likely that the primary focus will be indicated, intense individual services, that is, tier 3. At this time, wait lists for individual services can be addressed.

There are readily available resources that can be used to accomplish the activities in level 4, particularly the Center for Mental Health in Schools at UCLA. It is important to map systems for promoting health development, prevention, early intervention of emerging problems, as well as addressing existing chronic and severe problems. By planning for all levels of the continuum of services, *all* tiers of a population-based approach are addressed.

Level 5 establishes appropriate population-based programs at all tiers according to what was determined by the mapping activity in level 4. Prioritization of services and tiers is necessary, especially when there are competing needs. Level 5 also establishes monitoring/evaluation structures that are accountable to the service collaboration groups who are in turn accountable to the secretariat.

Level 6 is the reallocation, redeployment, and restructuring of school-based and community-based services according to what has been determined by the previous levels' activities. We realize that needs and resources are not static, so we have included a feedback loop to level 3, the Service Collaboration Group, as needs and resources change.

Moving toward improved ratios for school-based student support services would be a viable objective at this level. Chapter 5 summarized current research supporting school-based mental health services. We suggest that in many cases, community-based services and professionals will be redeployed to the schools.

Figure 7.3 depicts the collaboration of a small subset of schools and community organizations within a local school system. This represents a cross-section of the activities taking place in the lower circle in figure 7.1, addressing barriers to learning through SISSM. Normally, each school would have a core contingent of school-based student support professionals to manage the collaboration. Where this is not possible, a core group of school-based student support professionals can manage the collaboration in several schools.

We propose that the core group comprise at least two multidisciplinary professionals who have training in both mental health and school-based service delivery. Some jurisdictions' school-based programs consist of professionals from the fields of psychology, social work, and youth counselors. In other jurisdictions, there is a wider representation of school-based professionals in school-based programs, which also include allied health practitioners such as speech-language pathologists and occupational therapists.

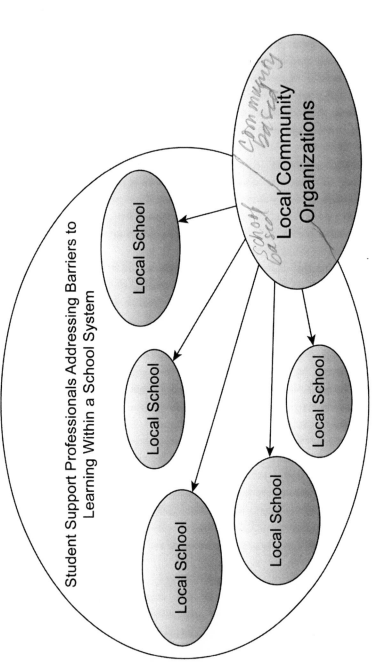

Figure 7.3. Collaboration of Schools and Community Organizations with Local School System through SISSM

The oval representing the community organizations is partially within the larger school system oval, showing that a portion of their services are redeployed and reallocated into the school system. The remaining portion of the community organizations' oval outside of the school system represents service to the broader community.

Figure 7.4 represents a more detailed depiction of the lower circle in figure 7.1, where we show how community organization services would be coordinated in a small subset of three schools. Notice that not all community organizations depicted in figure 7.2 are collaborating with each school. This reflects the diverse needs and resources previously mapped by the service collaboration group. It also reflects how services are reallocated and redeployed.

The core group of school-based student support professionals is key to the process of coordinating services in the schools. These professionals, through their support services roles, serve as a visible link and vital liaison with the community-based organizations that are collaborating with the school system to address barriers to learning.

School-based support services professionals play a more significant and broader role than before in addressing barriers to learning. This expanded collaborative support services team can now offer the continuum of programs required to provide a population-based approach.

The increase in student support professionals will make the goals of education reform and child and youth mental health reform more easily achievable. We caution, however, that the process of implementation will likely require several years to accomplish. Servicing high-demand tier 3 Indicated/Intensive needs is best reduced through a number of years of prevention and early intervention activities.

ADDRESSING ACADEMIC AND BEHAVIORAL/MENTAL HEALTH BARRIERS TO LEARNING THROUGH A POPULATION-BASED APPROACH[2]

The following section depicts how the population-based approach addresses academic and behavioral/mental health issues in schools by response to intervention (RTI) and positive behavioral supports (PBS). Figures 7.5 and 7.6 represent how SISSM's population-based approach would address academic and behavioral/mental health barriers to learning, respectively.

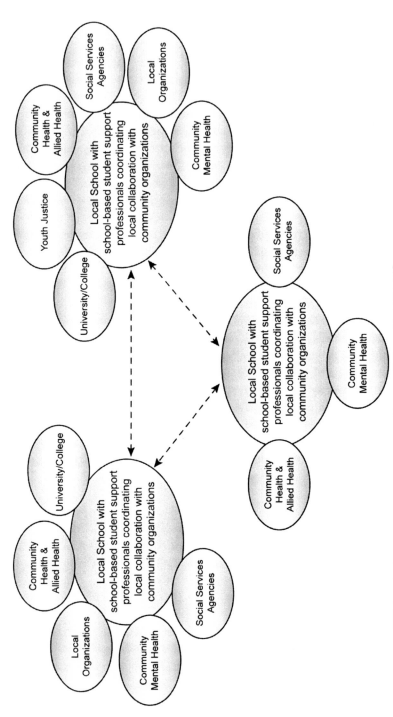

Figure 7.4. Example of Integrating Community Organization Services in Three Schools

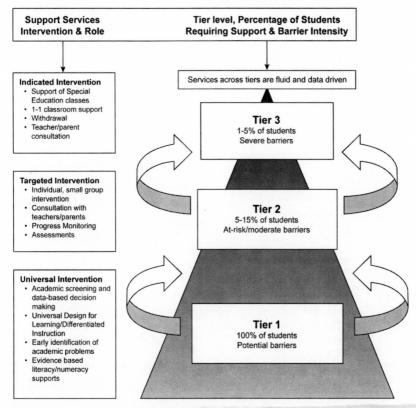

Figure 7.5. School-based Support Services Intervention and Role: Response to Intervention

Utilizing the SISSM approach, school-based support services and community organizations professionals collaborate to deliver the programs in each tier. School system–university/college collaborations can be especially helpful for universal screening activities in both PBS and RTI.

In contrast to figure 6.5, the inverted triangle, here support services professionals would implement programs in each tier, as illustrated in the triangles. Deployment of support services professionals would be determined by the service coordination group through the mapping activity.

Although we present RTI and PBS separately, they are interconnected and in practice should be viewed as such. For example, students presenting with behavior problems may have an undiagnosed learning disability that would require both behavior and academic supports.

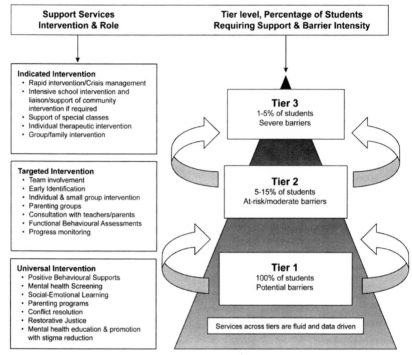

Figure 7.6.   School-based Support Services Intervention and Role: Positive Behavioral Supports

RESPONSE TO INTERVENTION (RTI)

Response to intervention begins with all students initially in tier 1. This Universal tier consists of all students' academic instruction based on research-supported techniques. All students' progress is measured at the beginning of the school year, often with curriculum-based assessments that can detect subtle levels of academic growth over short periods of time. If the students do not reach a predetermined level of achievement on the second set of these measures, they move on to tier 2.

In tier 2, the Targeted tier, students receive more intense instruction, sometimes by the classroom teacher and sometimes in a withdrawal or pullout evidence-based group program. The students' progress is measured more frequently, to determine if they are responding to the intervention.

After a predetermined time, a student's progress is examined. A decision is made to (1) continue the student in the tier 2 program, (2) return the student to a regular class program, or (3) refer the student to more intense supports, called tier 3, or Indicated Intervention.

Using this approach, intervention services can be more precisely offered. The untenable situation of students staying on waiting lists while they await services and intervention is therefore avoided. Research has shown that waiting lists tend to shorten with this approach.

POSITIVE BEHAVIORAL SUPPORTS (PBS)

Positive behavioral supports (PBS) provide a range of interventions at the earliest point possible with the overall goal of preventing problem behavior from occurring.

Tier 1, or Universal supports, is where all students are provided with a curriculum that involves schoolwide procedures, expectations, and rules to produce and maintain a safe and healthy school environment. This behavioral curriculum is often referred to as social emotional learning, and sometimes as character education. Students are taught and reinforced for exhibiting behavior in accordance with the school's expectations. Measures that screen for behavior or social emotional problems may be utilized.

In tier 2 in PBS, or Targeted support, students are identified as requiring additional support. Two methods of identifying these students are by the results of screening assessments that reach a predetermined cut-off point or by teacher nomination. The teaching and reinforcement programs in tier 1 would not be sufficient for these students. Measures may include a predetermined number of office discipline referrals. However, these referrals cannot identify students who have more "internalizing" behaviors, such as withdrawal, depression, or anxiety.

Screening measures are often utilized to detect students who internalize their behaviors. Many students do not participate in screening measures because of consent and confidentiality issues. Research and policy development is required in this area to address these issues.

PBS also requires assessing the classroom environment when determining whether a student had a positive response to a tier 1 or Universal intervention. As previously discussed in chapter 3, it can be difficult to determine if a student's behavior problem is internally based or related to the school environment. Schools systems must continually monitor the classroom and school environment to address these issues.

Examples of tier 2 supports include social skills groups and mentoring programs. Progress monitoring and overall evaluation of these programs is essential to their success. Research has shown that schools tend to implement programs that are familiar. These programs may lack empirical support, particularly with respect to efficacy and fidelity. Outcomes may not always be measured.

Although we have separated the discussions of academic and behavioral population-based approaches, as stated earlier, it is not advisable to separate them to address barriers to learning. The two areas are not mutually exclusive. In tier 2, it is extremely important to determine if behavioral problems are the result of academic problems, and, if this is the case, the academic problems need to be addressed.

Tier 3 supports occur after a student has not benefited from tier 2 interventions. Functional behavioral assessments may be used at this point to determine appropriate programming. An intervention plan is then implemented, and the student's response measured regularly. If the student does not improve, more intense interventions are applied, and consequently, more intense monitoring techniques are required.

CONTINUUM OF INTERVENTIONS IN POPULATION-BASED APPROACH TO BARRIERS TO LEARNING

Figure 7.7 expands the Universal, Targeted, and Indicated parts of a three-tiered approach and presents them in a continuous cycle. Universal supports are now divided into two categories: (1) evidence-based mental health promotion and academic instruction, and (2) universal prevention activities. Selected/Targeted approaches remain as a single part.

Indicated approaches expand to three categories: (1) indicated intervention activities that can most easily be carried out in the schools, (2) treatment intervention involves more specialized personnel and settings, and (3) management and chronic care, where interventions involve addressing chronic problems.

We present this graphic as a continuous cycle because as students' progress is measured, they are able to move from one level of intervention to another. Students who are progressing according to assessments can move to a less intense intervention. Students who are not progressing according to assessments can move to a more intense intervention. This cycle prevents students from remaining in one level receiving intervention that is not beneficial.

RESEARCHING THE EFFICACY OF SISSM[3]

SISSM is a model of service delivery that is designed to effectively and efficiently address barriers to learning. However, an in-depth evaluation of the model is required.

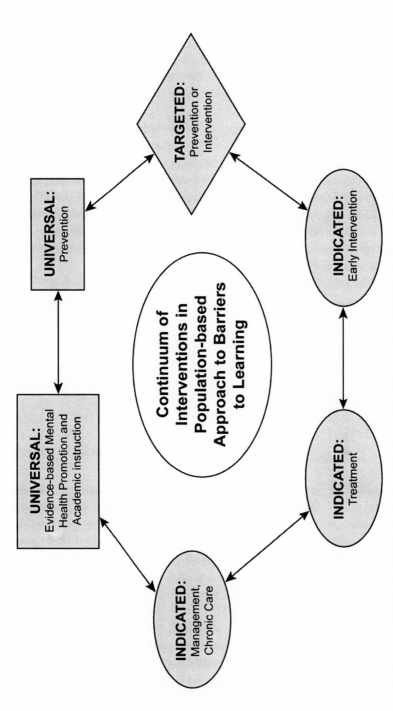

Figure 7.7. Continuum of Intervention in a Population-based Approach to Address Barriers to Learning

We suggest that pilot projects testing SISSM be conducted in selected sites in different school districts. Overall, several projects encompassing all six levels of the service continuum in figure 7.7 (both academic and mental health services) would need to be evaluated. Mixed-methods research is suggested, including case studies, service satisfaction ratings, and empirically based randomized controlled trials.

Multiple outcome measures, from both the education and mental health perspectives, should be utilized. These could include reduced symptoms in behavior and emotional areas, better outcomes in family relationships, increased academic achievement, and improved school climate and community functioning. Increases in protective factors, such as resiliency, can also be measured. Measures such as homework completion, participation in classroom discussions, problem-solving disputes with peers, and other areas would assist in developing useful interventions promoting better outcomes for children and youth.

When implementing population-based approaches, including SISSM, there are several cautions to consider. These cautions include the hazard of dominance of collaboration by one participating group (often a community mental health agency) and defining one participating group as a client or service recipient (often the school). We also caution that this process will likely take a number of years to implement and produce significant conclusive results. It is important, therefore, that attempts are not abandoned in early stages for lack of evidence.

SMALL-SCALE PILOT PROJECT IMPLEMENTATION GUIDE

A number of jurisdictions have successfully implemented collaborative school-community approaches to addressing barriers to learning. However, some jurisdictions may require locally produced evidence to support initiating a program of this nature. When implementing a trial of this kind of integrated system, we recommend that higher-level leaders from both a school board and local community organizations consider a small-scale trial that would include the following steps. School board and community leaders must:

1. Support the need for an integrated system, utilize a population-based approach, and have available sufficient school-based student support personnel to successfully implement SISSM.
2. Establish firm commitments from collaborative links (community organizations).
3. Include students and parents.

4. Include professional administrators of school-based support services' departments (e.g., supervising psychologist).
5. Include professional organizations and unions, where they exist.
6. Establish a common broad-based goal (generally defined as better outcomes for children and youth) and more specific goals depending on local needs.
7. Set leadership/organizational/governance/structure as stated in SISSM to be responsible for the implementation of programs.
8. Identify several sites in different districts/communities.
9. Map needs and resources in schools and community.
10. Reallocate and redeploy school-based and community-based professionals according to locally determined needs and resources after mapping exercises.
11. Define specific outcome measures:
    (a) school measures such as academic progress, office referrals, suspensions, detentions, absenteeism
    (b) clinical measures such as decreases in mental health symptoms.
12. Establish record-keeping systems that address differing confidentiality requirements in accordance with local legislation and standards of practice/ethics of each involved profession.
13. Set up, run, and evaluate programs. We suggest that, through the mapping program, one program at each tier of the population-based approach be implemented for both academic and mental health barriers to learning.
14. Cautions:
    (a) Consider that when changing to a population-based approach, several years may be required to produce significant change in outcome measures
    (b) Ensure that sufficient services exist so that they have significant impact
    (c) Ensure that existing support services not be removed when waiting lists dissipate

IDEAS TO CONSIDER

- School-based student support services professionals can be instrumental in providing a seamless delivery of services to ensure the best outcome for children and youth facing barriers to learning.

- School-based services should be mandated and broadened in order to effectively integrate the education and child and youth mental health systems through a population-based approach.
- In SISSM, a core group of school-based student support services personnel is vital to successfully provide integrated services for students.
- The "core group" component of SISSM is a major omission in other approaches that support community agencies colocating mental health services on school premises.
- SISSM should be implemented with a research component to evaluate the efficacy of the model.
- Several small-scale trials of SISSM may be necessary to provide sufficient evidence for large-scale implementation of the model.

EPILOGUE

ABC District School Board Revisited

Five years ago, child- and youth-serving governing bodies began to invest in an integrated service system culminating in a fully functioning School-based Integrated Support Services Model (SISSM). Through the Integrated Children and Youth Services Secretariat, ABC District School Board received funding to implement a population-based services approach to address barriers to learning.

This funding supported the establishment of an inaugural service collaboration group (SCG) that mapped local needs, services, and resources. The SCG determined that there was duplication and fragmentation of limited resources.

Services were reallocated and redeployed according to the determined needs that fit into a population-based approach. A combination of student support services professionals from schools and community organizations deliver a continuum of services ranging from mental health promotion to management of chronic problems. More services take place in school settings, which are coordinated by the core group of school-based support services professionals assigned to each school.

We examine the results of utilizing SISSM in the two fictional classes previously introduced in the prologue.

EFG ELEMENTARY SCHOOL:
MS. W.'S GRADE 3 CLASS

EFG Elementary is a school in ABC School District with a student population of 632. It is 9:08 a.m. on a Monday morning. The announcements are over. The class of twenty-five students takes several minutes to settle.

87

The teacher, Ms. W., begins her lesson by asking the class to take out their notebooks, pencils, and textbooks. The students begin their literacy block, which will take up the next hour and a half.

Ms. W. will implement a guided reading strategy and then the class will do independent reading and writing for the rest of the literacy block. Today, the independent writing assignment will involve a focus on nonfiction writing where the class will deconstruct an ad from the newspaper. Tomorrow, they will begin to use graphic organizers to help them learn to organize their thinking coherently.

The morning progresses smoothly, as Ms. W. utilizes differentiated instruction techniques to deal with the varied levels and learning styles of her students. She knows all her students' scores on the recent curriculum-based reading measurement; they are clearly displayed on the data wall in the primary level resource room. She has implemented high-yield strategies regularly discussed and reinforced at her school's primary level professional learning community.

Ms. W. uses continuous assessment and feedback as well as observations and other student data to inform her instruction. She has numerous student-teacher conferences and models and teaches metacognitive skills.

Ms. W. is pleased with the effects of the SISSM, utilizing PBS and RTI. The implementation of the SISSM approach has allowed EFG School to be able to respond to the needs of students more efficiently. Identifying and responding to students facing barriers to learning earlier has reduced the number of students requiring intensive intervention.

Beth was diagnosed with a severe learning disability and anxiety by the school psychologist shortly after her academic difficulties became apparent. Beth has shown many improvements by participating in several interventions at school following her diagnosis. These interventions include a number of collaborative programs managed by the school-based psychologist. Beth is participating in cognitive behavior therapy for her anxiety from the school-based psychologist. She also participates in a group metacognitive strategy training program delivered by the school-linked psychologist and a graduate student from the local university.

Carl is doing his seat work. Carl was flagged in kindergarten as a student requiring intervention because he was unable to sit still, work independently, or get along with his peers and teachers. The school support services team met several times with Carl's parents to discuss his difficulties in the classroom. The school-based psychologist diagnosed him with attention deficit hyperactivity disorder in grade 1.

Through SISSM, a referral to a school-linked pediatrician specializing in attention disorders was made and medication was prescribed. Carl's medication levels are closely monitored by the school-based psychologist in consultation with the pediatrician. Additional intervention includes the cognitive training program delivered by school-linked university researchers.

After Carl's diagnosis, his parents participated in programs specifically for parents of students with attention disorders. These programs were run by the school-based social worker and a school-linked social worker from a social service agency. The programs were helpful; however, they were not able to address certain family issues. The family is now participating in family therapy, which is provided at the school by the school-based social worker and a school-linked psychologist.

Billy is at his desk doing his work. Billy was screened in grade 1 for behavior and academic concerns. He was placed in a tier 2 mental health prevention program where he learned coping and resilience skills in a play-based approach. He was also withdrawn twice weekly for academic supports in a small group. The interventions were successful; however, he is still closely monitored.

Kyle returns to class. He is participating in an intervention program run by a local hospital for families dealing with mental illnesses. He is returning to class from a session run by the school-based social worker and a school-linked child and youth counselor. His attendance has improved significantly and he is making good academic progress. His mother is also making progress by participating regularly in the family intervention program that takes place at school. This is in addition to the individual treatment she receives at the hospital.

Meanwhile, Robin is returning to class with his educational resource worker, Mrs. S. She removed him from the classroom to work with him individually. Robin is a child with a rare chromosomal disorder that has the following effects: a severe intellectual disability, poor muscle tone, small stature, and challenging behaviors. His receptive language skills, although low, are better than his minimal expressive language skills. Robin also has a high activity level and can only stay seated and focused for a short period of time.

Ms. W. and Mrs. S., as well as Robin's parents, are now able to predict his frustration levels with more accuracy after the school-based psychologist implemented a functional behavioral assessment. Robin is currently being taught to use an augmentative communication system by a school-based speech-language pathologist. The school-based psychologist regularly meets with Ms. W., Mrs. S., and Robin's parents to monitor his behavioral program.

His aggressive outbursts are rapidly decreasing and he is developing more appropriate social skills.

Ms. W. notices that Ross is hard at work on his task. He no longer requires tier 2 progress monitoring, although in grade 1, he was not progressing at the expected rate in reading. These academic difficulties were identified through the schoolwide progress monitoring assessment portion of the Response to Intervention program. These assessments were administered by school-linked graduate students from the local university. He was given class-based intervention recommended by consultation with the school support team, responded well, and has not had any further problems.

Cindy returns to the classroom from her tier 2 program. Cindy did not progress will with the school's tier 1 Positive Behavior Support program. All of Ms. W.'s students were screened at the beginning of the year on measures of independence, attention, and mood. Cindy's scores on this screening measure determined that she would be a good candidate for a tier 2 program that supports students who are having difficulties with school adjustment. This particular program offers students twelve weeks of individual play-based and child-led sessions with a teaching assistant, supervised by the school-based psychologist. Cindy is benefiting from the program. Since she began several weeks ago, she has not been sent to the office for aggressive outbursts.

Ms. W. sees that both Cameron and Jamie have their hands up. As a result of education reforms, including the implementation of SISSM, Ms. W. is able to address requests for assistance from Cameron, Jamie, and other students who are not facing barriers to learning.

XYZ SECONDARY SCHOOL:
MR. M.'S GRADE 10 ENGLISH CLASS

XYZ Secondary School is a midsized high school in ABC School District. Mr. M. is an English teacher. He teaches three classes in a two semester system; one grade 12 university stream class, one grade 10 junior college stream class, and a grade 11 class for students going into the world of work.

Mr. M. is pleased with the effects of the universally administered Positive Behavior Support program at his school. The implementation of the SISSM approach has allowed XYZ School to be able to respond to the needs of students and their families more efficiently. This is accomplished by identifying and responding to academic and behavior problems earlier, and effectively reducing the number of students with high needs. In fact, fewer problems in these areas are surfacing, because they are often addressed earlier at the elementary level.

Mr. M. is marking term papers while his grade 10 junior college stream class works on an assignment. Many students are doing well in the course and are able to work independently. For example, two students with learning disabilities are taking advantage of the special software package provided by the school. He has noticed that their writing skills have improved considerably.

A paper from George, a student who failed his last semester, is well done. The paper reflects the additional support provided to him and other students through recent education department academic initiatives. As a result, George is much more motivated to learn, his achievement in his other courses has increased, and he is less disruptive in class.

The next paper is from Rena. Rena was diagnosed with depression and has been treated by the school-based psychologist shortly after universal screening was administered in grade 9. She is on medication prescribed by her school-linked family doctor. He regularly interacts with the school-based student support services team, ensuring that Rena's condition is closely monitored.

Mr. M. and his colleagues feel more confident teaching students with mental health issues. This is a result of regular in-services provided by school-based and school-linked professionals. These in-services include antistigma training and universal mental health promotion. These interventions have also made it easier for students like Rena to understand and accept their condition while feeling more connected with the school.

Mr. M. reads Jessica's paper. She has a long history of anxiety, but it has always been treated through school-based services. Although the intensity of her symptoms varies, she has always been able to access more intense intervention when required. A combination of school-based and school-linked student support services monitor her closely.

The next paper is from Evan. Evan is a student with a learning disability that was diagnosed in grade 5. As a result of the implementation of SISSM, school-based and school-linked support services were able to provide the necessary supports that Evan and his family required. He is doing well and is looking forward to a postsecondary education.

Jayden's paper reflects the progress he has made. He was assessed by the school-based psychologist in grade 6 and found to be gifted and learning disabled. He was placed in a program for students who are gifted and have learning disabilities. Additionally, he has had school-linked occupational therapy services, which, along with the provision of assistive technology, have successfully addressed his written language difficulties. His attention problems diminished markedly with these interventions.

Bryan's paper is also well done. Bryan's father is on disability and his mother works long hours at the local donut shop; therefore, Bryan has to work to help his family financially. The school-based social worker arranged for Bryan to work in a paid coop placement in a school-linked after-school recreation program. This program provides part-time employment as well as the necessary experience to assist Bryan in his pursuit of a diploma in community recreation.

Ray's paper continues to raise concerns about both his schoolwork and well-being. Mr. M. suspects that Ray is abusing substances. Mr. M. has attempted to contact Ray's parents, but his efforts have proven to be unsuccessful. The school-based social worker has met with Ray and his parents several times with limited progress. Ray was referred to the school-linked harm reduction program but refused to attend.

As a result of more efficient collaboration with community organizations, Ray is successfully referred to a residential addiction treatment program by the school-based and school-linked student support team.

Mr. M. observes that Patrick and Chase have handed in good papers. Patrick is progressing well in a classroom that is free of most disruptions and tension. Chase's paper is well done. After the school adopted positive behavior supports and an antibullying program, Chase no longer feels victimized. He is confident and more socially accepted by his peers than when he first enrolled at the school.

The implementation of SISSM by the ABC District School Board has facilitated the collaboration of school-based and school-linked community organizations. Ms. W., Mr. M., and their colleagues in ABC School District have benefited greatly from the SISSM approach that the board and the local community organizations implemented five years ago to address all barriers to learning.

The implementation of SISSM in the past five years has resulted in more efficient and effective collaboration between school-based and school-linked student support services. When the needs of all students are addressed through a population-based approach, teachers are free to teach, and students are free to learn.

CONCLUSION

We have presented the case for integrated school-based support services to address barriers to learning. With the understanding that all students are connected in some manner with schools, we developed the School-based Integrated Support Services Model (SISSM) as a framework for timely and evidence-based integrated and collaborative services for children and youth experiencing barriers to learning.

Reaching all students is crucial when statistics state that up to 20 percent of children and youth have mental health issues and up to 80 percent do not receive any intervention, or receive inadequate intervention. We hypothesize that learning can be compromised for students in the classroom who are not facing barriers to learning as a result of the Multi-Ripple Effect.

Within the context of exceptional school leadership and instruction, and a population-based approach, SISSM advocates for a pivotal, central role for school-based student support services professionals. In addition to direct service to students, educators, and parents, these school-based professionals can function in a core role to manage the collaboration of the school system and the external community organizations who deal with children and youth.

Services to students, families, and schools are provided with locally determined variations of integrated collaborations between professional school-based services and community organization professionals. A core group of school-based board-employed student support services professionals are pivotal in coordinating services, supporting academic achievement, and meeting students' mental health needs.

Services encompass a population-based continuum including social emotional learning; mental health promotion, prevention, early intervention, and treatment; and management of environmental-circumstantial barriers by building resilience and promoting protective factors.

A coordinated, collaborative, and integrated system for servicing students facing barriers to learning is necessary as well as timely. The implementation of SISSM has the potential to close the achievement gap while integrating mental health services for children and youth.

NOTES

PROLOGUE

1. The term *psychologists* is used here as a generic term for clarity. Different jurisdictions use various terms to refer to professionals with one or more postgraduate degrees in psychology that are registered to practice and perform controlled acts such as diagnosis of mental disorders.

CHAPTER 1

1. Phelps, Brown & Power (2002)
2. Breton et al. (1999)
3. U.S. Department of Health and Human Services (U.S. DHSS) (1999)

CHAPTER 2

1. Learning Disabilities:
   a. Dillon (2007)
   b. Flagle (2008)
   c. American Psychiatric Association (2000)
   d. Bowman (2002)
   e. Boudah & Weiss (2002)
   f. Learning Disabilities Association of Ontario (2008)
   g. Canadian Council on Social Development (2001)
   h. Margai & Henry (2003)
   i. Levine (2001)
   j. Nielson (2002)

2. Attention Deficit Hyperactivity Disorders:
   a. American Psychiatric Association (2000)
   b. O'Connell (2006)
   c. Clark, Prior, & Kinsella (2002)
   d. Tannock & Martinussen (2001)
   e. Martinussen & Tannock (2006)
   f. Stein et al. (2002)
   g. American Psychiatric Association (2000)
   h. U.S. DHHS (1999)
   i. Waddell et al. (2005)
   j. Bowman (2002)
   k. Rowland et al. (2001)
   l. Barkely (2006)
   m. CADDRA (2008)
   n. American Academy of Child and Adolescent Psychiatry (2007)
   o. Havey, Olson, & McCormick (2005)
   p. CADDRA (2008)
   q. American Academy of Pediatrics (2001)
   r. Hale et al. (1998)
   s. Fiorello & Hyman (1998)
   t. DuPaul (1992)
3. Anxiety Disorders
   a. Cartwright-Hatton et al. (2006)
   b. U.S. DHHS (1999)
   c. Waddell et al. (2005)
   d. Langley, Bergman, & Piacentini (2002)
   e. Chavira et al. (2004)
   f. American Psychiatric Association (2000)
   g. U.S. DHHS (1999)
   h. American Psychiatric Association (2000)
   i. U.S. DHHS (1999)
   j. American Psychiatric Association (2000)
   k. U.S. DHHS (1999)
   l. American Psychiatric Association (2000)
   m. Bokszczanin (2006)
   n. Kilpatrick et al. (2003)
   o. Kinzie (2006)
4. Mood Disorders
   a. Reber (2002)
   b. American Psychiatric Association (2000)
   c. U.S. DHHS (1999)
   d. Waddell et al. (2005)
   e. Costello, Erkanli, & Angold (2006)

    f. Breton et al. (1999)

    g. Canadian Psychiatric Research Foundation (2004)

    h. Reber (2002)

    i. American Psychiatric Association (2000)

    j. Blader (2007)

    k. Coghlan (2007)

    l. American Psychiatric Association (2000)

5. Disruptive Disorders

    a. American Psychiatric Association (2000)

    b. Wolff & Ollendick (2006)

    c. Nock et al. (2007)

    d. U.S. DHHS (1999)

6. Slow Learners

    a. Shaw (1999)

7. Speech and Language Disorders

    a. Stuart (2002)

    b. Choudhury & Benasich (2003)

    c. American Psychiatric Association (2000)

    d. Beitchman et al. (1996)

    e. Snowling et al. (2006)

8. Developmental Disabilities

    a. American Psychiatric Association (2000)

    b. Batshaw & Shapiro (2002)

    c. Reber (2002)

9. Autism Spectrum Disorders

    a. American Psychiatric Association (2000)

    b. Nicholas et al. (2008)

    c. American Psychiatric Association (2000)

    d. U.S. DHHS (1999)

    e. Waddell et al. (2005)

    f. Fombonne (2005)

    g. Wazana, Bresnahan, & Kline (2007)

    h. Taubin, Mauk, & Batshaw (2002)

    i. de Bruin (2007)

10. Tic Disorders

    a. American Psychiatric Association (2000)

    b. Singer (2005)

11. Prenatal Maternal Substance Abuse

    a. Wunsch, Conlon, & Scheidt (2002)

12. Eating Disorders

    a. U.S. DHHS (1999)

    b. Ackard, Fulkerson, & Neumark-Sztainer (2007)

    c. Waddell et al. (2005)

13. Selective Mutism
    a. Chavira et al. (2004)
    b. Kumpulainen (2002)
    c. American Psychiatric Association (2000)
14. Sensory Disorders—Blind and Low Vision and Deaf and Hard-of-Hearing
    a. Wall & Corn (2004)
    b. Hener, Knightly, & Steinberg (2002)
15. Chronic and Life-Threatening Illness
    a. Hewitt, Weiner, & Simone (2003)
    b. Nabors & Lehmkuhl (2004)

CHAPTER 3

1. Children and Youth Exposed to Domestic Violence
    a. Fantuzzo & Fusco (2007)
    b. Roberts (2006)
    c. Spilsbury et al. (2008)
    d. Brown & Bzostek (2003)
    e. Onyskiw (2007)
2. Child Abuse
    a. Hussey, Chang, & Kotch (2006)
    b. Black et al. (2008)
    c. Goldman et al. (2003)
3. Change in Family Constitution
    a. Conway (2003)
    b. Jenkins et al. (2005)
4. Social Discrimination
    a. Coll & Szalacha (2004)
5. Economic Challenges
    a. UNICEF (2007)
    b. Wadsworth, Raviv, & Reinhard (2008)
6. Loss of Job/Unemployment
    a. MacMillan & Violato (2008)
7. Mass Media
    a. Rideout (2007)
    b. Roberts, Foehr, & Rideout (2005)
    c. Brown & Bzostek (2003)
8. Barriers to Learning and Labeling
    a. Adelman & Taylor (2006)

CHAPTER 4

1. Bullying
   a. Olweus (1993)
   b. Beran & Tutty (2002)
   c. Mishna, Pepler, & Weiner (2006)
   d. Pepler et al. (2006)
   e. Mishna, Pepler, & Weiner (2006)
   f. Adlaf et al. (2005)
   g. Beran & Tutty (2002)
   h. Dehue, Bolman, & Völlink (2008)
   i. Kowalski & Limber (2007)
2. School Refusal
   a. Kearney (2007)
   b. Kearney (2008)
   c. Henry (2007)
3. Early School Leaving/Dropouts
   a. Christle, Jolivette, & Nelson (2007)
   b. Neild, Stoner-Eby, & Furstenberg (2008)
   c. Robertson (2006)
   d. Neild, Balfranz, & Herzog (2007)
4. Addictions
   a. U.S. DHHS (1999)
   b. Kilpatrick et al. (2003)
   c. Adlaf & Paglia-Boak (2007)
   d. Adlaf et al. (2005)
   e. Adlaf & Paglia-Boak (2007)
5. Suicide
   a. Adlaf et al. (2005)
   b. Waldrop et al. (2007)
   c. Mazza & Reynolds (2008)
   d. Rosenberg et al. (2006)
   e. Pelkonen & Marttnunen (2003)
   f. Fotti et al. (2006)
   g. Ackard et al. (2006)
6. Youth Violence
   a. McMurtry & Curling (2008)
   b. Brown & Bzostek (2003)
   c. Jerrom (2003)
   d. Koller & Bertel (2006)
   e. Christle, Nelson, & Jolivette (2008)

7. The Multi-Ripple Effect
   a. Rones & Hoagwood (2000)
   b. Paternité & Johnston (2005)
   c. Daly et al. (2006)
   d. Coalition for Psychology in Schools and Education (2006)
   e. Alvarez (2007)

CHAPTER 5

1. Education Reform and Barriers to Learning
   a. Darling-Hammond, Ancess, & Orr (2002)
   b. Fullan, Hill, & Crévola (2006)
   c. Blankstein (2004)
   d. Hargreaves & Shirley (2009)
   e. Center for Mental Health in Schools (2008b)
2. Government Initiatives in Education Reform
   a. U.S. Department of Education (2002)
   b. Ontario Ministry of Education (2008b)
3. Government Initiatives in Special Education Reform
   a. Kutash, Duchnowski, & Lynn (2006)
   b. Ringeisen, Henderson, & Hoagwood (2003)
   c. Lerner & Johns (2008)
   d. Ontario Ministry of Education (2001)
   e. Ontario Ministry of Education (2006)
   f. Daly et al. (2006)
   g. Neuman (2008)
   h. Canadian Psychological Association (2002a, 2002b)
   i. Saklofske et al. (2007)
   j. Koller & Bertel (2006)
4. Alternative Education and Barriers to Learning
   a. Paternité et al. (2008)
5. Child and Youth Mental Health Reform and the Role of Schools
   a. Phelps, Brown, & Power (2002)
   b. Isaacs (2006)
   c. Pumariega & Vance (1999)
   d. President's New Freedom Commission on Mental Health (2003)
   e. Koller & Bertel (2006)
   f. Waddell et al. (2005)
   g. Wagner (2005)
   h. U.S. DHSS (1999)
   i. President's New Freedom Commission on Mental Health (2003)

j. Kirby & Keon (2006)
k. Carnegie Council (1989)
l. Paternité & Johnston (2005)
m. Adelman & Taylor (2006)
n. Zins et al. (2004)
o. Rones & Hoagwood (2000)
p. Masia-Warner, Nangle, & Hansen (2006)
q. Vanderbleek (2004)
r. Crisp, Gudmundsen, & Shirk (2006)
s. Massey et al. (2005)
t. Atkins et al. (2003)
u. Bruns et al. (2005)

CHAPTER 6

1. Limitations of School System Methods for Addressing Barriers to Learning
   a. American Academy of Pediatrics Committee on School Health (2004)
   b. Blank (2004)
   c. Brown & Bolen (2003)
   d. Slade (2003)
2. Population-Based Approaches to Addressing Barriers to Learning
   a. Kutash et al. (2006)
   b. Doll & Cummings (2008b)
3. Common Approach to Addressing Barriers to Learning: The Inverted Triangle
   a. Center for Mental Health in Schools (2008a)
4. Advantages of School-Based Support Services Implementing a Population-Based Approach to Address Barriers to Learning
   a. Center for Mental Health in Schools (2008a)
   b. Heathfield & Clark (2004)
5. Research on Population-Based Approaches to Addressing Barriers to Learning
   a. DeBeer & Gairey (2008)
   b. Weist et al. (2007)

CHAPTER 7

1. Implementation of Population-Based Services to Address Barriers to Learning: SISSM
   a. Center for Mental Health in Schools (2007a)

2. Addressing Academic and Behavioral/Mental Health Barriers to Learning through a Population-Based Approach
   a. McCook (2006)
   b. Bender & Shores (2007)
   c. Zins et al. (2004)
   d. Ontario Ministry of Education (2006)
3. Researching the Efficacy of SISSM
   a. Center for Mental Health in Schools (2008a)
   b. Doll & Cummings (2008a, 2008b)

REFERENCES

Abel, E. L. (2006). Fetal alcohol syndrome: A cautionary note. *Current Pharmaceutical Design, 12,* 1521–1529.

Ackard, D. M., Fulkerson, J. A., & Neumark-Sztainer, D. (2007). Prevalence and utility of DSM-IV eating disorder diagnostic criteria among youth. *International Journal of Eating Disorders, 40(5),* 409–417.

Ackard, D. M., Neumark-Sztainer, D., Story, M., & Perry, C. (2006). Parent-child connectedness and behavioral and emotional health among adolescents. *American Journal of Preventative Medicine, 30(1),* 59–66.

Adelman, H., & Taylor, L. (2006). *The Implementation Guide to Student Learning Supports in the Classroom and Schoolwide: New Directions for Addressing Barriers to Learning.* Thousand Oaks, CA: Corwin Press.

Adlaf, E. M., & Paglia-Boak, A. (2007). *Drug Use among Ontario Students: 1977–2007. CAMH Research Document Series No. 21.* Toronto: Centre for Addiction and Mental Health.

Adlaf, E. M., Paglia-Boak, A., Beitchman, J. H., & Wolfe, D. (2005). *The Mental Health and Well-being of Ontario Students: CAMH Research Document Series No. 18,* Toronto: Centre for Addiction and Mental Health.

Alvarez, H. K. (2007). Teachers' thinking about classroom management: The explanatory role of self-reported psychosocial characteristics. *Advances in School Mental Health, 1(1),* 42–54.

American Academy of Child and Adolescent Psychiatry (2007). Practice parameter for the assessment and treatment of children and adolescents with attention-deficit/hyperactivity disorder. *Journal of the American Academy of Child and Adolescent Psychiatry, 46(7),* 894–921.

American Academy of Pediatrics Committee on School Health. (2004). School-based mental health services. *Pediatrics, 113,* 1839–1845.

American Academy of Pediatrics, Subcommittee on ADHD and Committee on Quality Improvement. (2001). Clinical practice guideline: Diagnosis and evaluation of the school-aged child with attention-deficit/hyperactivity disorder. *Pediatrics, 105,* 1158–1170.

American Psychiatric Association (2000). *Diagnostic and Statistical Manual of Mental Disorders* (4th ed., Text rev.). Washington, DC: Author.

Anderson-Butcher, D., Stetler, E.G., & Midle, T. (2006). A case for expanded school-community partnerships in support of positive youth development. *Children and Schools, 28(3),* 155–163.

Apter, A., & King, R.A. (2006). Management of the depressed, suicidal child or adolescent. *Child and Adolescent Psychiatric Clinics of North America, 15(4),* 999–1013.

Atkins, M. S., Graczyk, P. A., Frazier, S. L., & Abdul-Adil, J. (2003). Toward a new model for promoting urban children's mental health: Accessible, effective, and sustainable school-based mental health services. *School Psychology Review, 12(4),* 503–514.

Auster, E. R., Feeney-Kettler, K. A., & Kratochwill, T. R. (2006). Conjoint behavioral consultation: Application to the school-based treatment of anxiety disorders. *Education and Treatment of Children, 29(2),* 243–256.

Australian Government Department of Health and Ageing. (2007). *KidsMatter—Australian Primary Schools Mental Health Initiative: Overview.* Canberra, ACT: Author.

Baggerly, J., & Exum, H. A. (2008). Counselling children after natural disasters: Guidance for family therapists. *American Journal of Family Therapy, 36(3),* 79–93.

Baker, J. A. (2008). Assessing school risk and protective factors. In B. Doll & J.A. Cummings (Eds.), *Transforming School Mental Health Services: Population-based Approaches to Promoting the Competency and Wellness of Children.* (pp. 43–65). Thousand Oaks, CA: Corwin Press.

Barkely, R. A. (2006). *Attention Deficit Hyperactivity Disorder: A Handbook of Diagnosis and Treatment* (3rd ed.). New York: Guilford Press.

Batshaw, M. L., & Shapiro, B. (2002). Mental retardation. In M.L. Batshaw (Ed.), *Children with Disabilities* (pp. 287–305). Baltimore, MD: Paul H. Brooks Publishing Co.

Beitchman, J. H., Cohen, M., Konstantareas, M., & Tannock, R. (Eds.). (1996). *Language, Learning and Behavior Disorders.* Cambridge: Cambridge University Press.

Bender. W. N., & Shores, C. (2007). *Response to Intervention: A Practical Guide for Teachers.* Thousand Oaks, CA: Corwin Press.

Beran, T. N. & Tutty, L. (2002). Children's reports of bullying and safety at school. *Canadian Journal of Psychology, 17(2),* 1–14.

Bickham, N. L., Pizarro, L. J., Warner, B. S., Rosenthal, B., & Weist, M. D. (1998). Family involvement in expanded school mental health. *Journal of School Health, 68(10),* 425–428.

Bierman, K. L. (2003). Commentary: New models for school-based mental health services. *School Psychology Review, 32(4),* 525–529.

Black, T., Trocmé, N., Fallon, B., & MacLaurin, B. (2008). The Canadian child welfare system response to exposure to domestic violence investigations. *Child Abuse & Neglect, 32(3),* 393–404.

Blader, J. C. (2007). Increased rates of bipolar disorder diagnoses among U.S. child, adolescent and adult inpatients 1996–2004. *Biological Psychiatry, 62(2),* 107–114.

Blanchard, L. T. (2006). Emotional, developmental and behavioral health of American children and their families: A report from the 2003 National Survey of Children's Health. *Pediatrics, 117(6),* 1202–1212.

Blank, M. J. (2004). How community schools make a difference. *Educational Leadership, 61(8),* 62–65.

Blankstein, A. M. (2004). *Failure Is Not an Option: Six Principles That Guide Student Achievement in High-Performing Schools.* Thousand Oaks, CA: Corwin Press.

Bokszczanin, A. (2006). PTSD symptoms in children and adolescents 28 months after a flood: Age and gender differences. *Journal of Traumatic Stress, 20(3),* 347–351.

Boudah, D. J., & Weiss, M. P. (2002). Learning disability overview: Update 2002. *ERIC Digest, ED4628082002–01–00,* 1–7.

Bowman, D. H. (2002). National survey puts ADHD incidence near 7 percent. *Education Week, 21(38).*

Brener, N. D., Weist, M. D., Adelman, H., Taylor, L., & Vernon-Smiley, M. (2007). Mental health and social services: Results from the school health policies and program study 2006. *Journal of School Health, 77(6),* 486–499.

Breton, J., Bergeron, L., Valla, J., Berthiaume, C., Gaudet, N., Lambert, J., St-Georges, M., Houde, L., & Lépine, S. (1999). Quebec child mental health survey: Prevalence of DSM-III-R mental health disorders. *Journal of Child Psychology and Psychiatry, 40(3),* 375–384.

Brown, B. V., & Bzostek, S. (2003). Violence in the lives of children. *Cross Currents, Child Trends Databank, 1,* 1–13.

Brown, M. B., & Bolen, L. M. (2003). School-based health centers: Stategies for meeting the physical and mental health needs of children and families. *Psychology in the Schools, 40(3),* 279–287.

Bruns, E. J., Moore, E., Stephan, S. H., Pruitt, D., & Weist, M. D. (2005). The impact of school mental health services on out-of-school suspension rates. *Journal of Youth and Adolescence, 34(1),* 23–30.

Buysse, V., Sparkman, K. L., & Wesley, P. W. (2003). Communities of Practice: Connecting what we know with what we do. *Exceptional Children, 69(3),* 263–278.

Cambra, C. (2005). Feelings and emotions in deaf adolescents. *Deafness and Education International, 7(4),* 195–205.

Canadian ADHD Resource Alliance (CADDRA). Canadian ADHD Practice Guidelines. Retrieved January 19, 2008, from www.caddra.ca/english/phys_guide.html.

Canadian Council on Social Development. (2001). Children and youth with special needs: Summary report of findings. Ottawa: Author.

Canadian Psychiatric Research Foundation. (2004). *When Something's Wrong: Strategies for Teachers*. Toronto: Author.

Canadian Psychological Association. (2002a). *Enhancing the Experience of Children and Youth in Today's Schools: The Role of Psychology in Canadian Schools—A Position Paper*. Ottawa: Author.

———. (2002b). *Enhancing the Experience of Children and Youth in Today's Schools: The Role of Psychology in Canadian Schools—The Contribution of the School Psychologist*. Ottawa: Author.

Carnegie Council on Adolescent Development Task Force on the Education of Young Adolescents. (1989). *Turning Points: Preparing American Youth for the 21st Century*. New York: Author.

Cartwright-Hatton, S., McNicol, K., & Doubleday, E. (2006). Anxiety in a neglected population: Prevalence of anxiety disorders in preadolescent children. *Clinical Psychology Review, 26(7)*, 817–833.

Center for Mental Health in Schools at UCLA. (2006). *Where's It Happening? Examples of New Directions for Student Support and Lessons Learned*. Los Angeles: Author.

———. (2007a). *A Resource Aid Packet on Addressing Barriers to Learning: A Set of Surveys to Map What a School Has and What It Needs*. Los Angeles: Author.

———. (2007b). *Framing New Directions for Schools Counselors, Psychologists and Social Workers*. Los Angeles: Author.

———. (2008a). *Conduct and Behavior Problems Related to School Aged Youth*. Los Angeles: Author.

———. (2008b). *Mental Health in Schools and School Improvement: Current Status, Concerns and New Directions*. Los Angeles: Author.

Chartier, M., Stoep, A. V., McCauley, E., Herting, J. R., Tracy, M., & Lymp, J. (2008). Passive versus active parental permission: Implications for the ability of school-based depression screening to reach youth at risk. *Journal of School Health, 78(3)*, 157–164.

Chavira, D. A., Stein, M. B., Bailey, K. &, Stein, M. T. (2004). Childhood anxiety in primary care: Prevalent but untreated. *Depression and Anxiety, 20*, 155–164.

Choudhury, N., & Benasich, A. A. (2003). A family aggregation study: The influence of family history and other risk factors on language development. *Journal of Speech, Language and Hearing Research, 46*, 261–272.

Christle, C. A., Jolivette, K. & Nelson, C. M. (2007). School characteristics related to school dropout rates. *Remedial and Special Education, 28(6)*, 325–339.

Christle, C. A., Nelson, C. M., & Jolivette, K. (2008). Prevention of antisocial and violent behavior in youth: A review of the literature. Retrieved February 8, 2008, from www.edff.org/focus/prevention/plr.pdf.

Clark, C., Prior, M., & Kinsella, G. (2002). The relationship between executive function abilities, adaptive behavior, and academic achievement in children with externalizing behavior problems. *Journal of Child Psychology and Psychiatry, 43*, 785–796.

Coalition for Psychology in Schools and Education. (2006). Report on the teacher needs survey. Washington, DC: American Psychological Association, Centre for Psychology in Schools and Education.

Coghlan, A. (2007). Young and moody or mentally ill? *New Scientist, 194(2604),* 6–7.

Coll, C. G., & Szalacha, L. A. (2004). The multiple contexts of middle childhood. *Future of Children, 14(2),* 81–97.

Conway, J. F. (2003). *The Canadian Family in Crisis* (5th ed.). Toronto: James Lorimer and Company.

Costello, E. J., Erkanli, A., & Angold, A. (2006). Is there an epidemic of child and adolescent depression? *Journal of Child Psychology and Psychiatry, 47(12),* 1263–1271.

Crisp, H. L., Gudmundsen, G. R., & Shirk, S. R. (2006). Transporting evidence-based therapy for adolescent depression to the school setting. *Education and Treatment of Children, 29(2),* 287–309.

Daly, B. P., Burke, R., Hare, I., Mills, C., Owens, C., Moore, E., & Weist, M. D. (2006). Enhancing No Child Left Behind: School mental health connections. *Journal of School Health, 76(9),* 446–451.

Darling-Hammond, L., Ancess, J., & Orr, S.W. (2002). Reinventing high school: Outcomes of the Coalition Campus Schools Project. *American Educational Review Journal, 30,* 639–673.

Davis, A. S., Kruczek, T., & McIntosh, D. E. (2006). Understanding and treating psychopathology in the schools: Introduction to the special issue. *Psychology in the Schools, 43(4),* 413–417.

DeBeer, Y., & Gairey, J. D. (2008). Enhancing services: Enhancing success. Improved outcomes for all students: Enhancing the role of professional and para-professional student support service practitioners. Toronto: Ontario Secondary School Teachers' Federation.

De Bruin, E. (2007). High rates of co-morbidity in PDD-NOS. *Journal of Autism and Developmental Disorders, 37(5),* 877–886.

Dehue, F., Bolman, C., & Völlink, T. (2008). Cyberbullying: Youngsters' experiences and parental perception. *CyberPsychology & Behavior, 11(2),* 217–223.

Dillon, E. (2007). Charts you can trust. Labeled: The students behind NCLB's "disabilities" designation. *Education Sector Digest.* Retrieved July 29, 2008, from www.educationsector.org/analysis/analysis_show.htm?doc_id=509392.

Doll, B., & Cummings, J. A. (2008a). Getting from here to there. In B. Doll & J.A. Cummings (Eds.), *Transforming School Mental Health Services: Population-based Approaches to Promoting the Competency and Wellness of Children.* (pp 307–334). Thousand Oaks, CA: Corwin Press.

———. (2008b). Why population-based services are essential for school mental health, and how to make them happen in your school. In B. Doll & J.A. Cummings (Eds.), *Transforming School Mental Health Services: Population-based Ap-*

proaches to *Promoting the Competency and Wellness of Children*. (pp 1–20). Thousand Oaks, CA: Corwin Press.

Druschel, C. M. (2007). Issues in estimating the prevalence of fetal alcohol syndrome: Examination of 2 counties in New York State. *Pediatrics, 119(2),* 384–390.

DuPaul, G. J. (1991). How to assess Attention-Deficit Hyperactivity Disorder within school settings. *School Psychology Quarterly,* 7, 45–58.

Fantuzzo, J., & Fusco, R. (2007). Children's direct exposure to types of domestic violence crime: A population-based investigation. *Journal of Family Violence, 22(7),* 543–552.

Fiorello, C. A., & Hyman, I.A. (1998). Monitoring medication response in attention disorders: Methodological issues. *Journal of Learning Disabilities, 31(6),* 579–580.

Flagle, R. (2008). Summary information about students placed in special education. Retrieved July 29, 2008, from www.seformmatrix.com/raven/index.htm.

Fombonne, E. (2005). The changing epidemiology of autism. *Journal of Applied Research in Intellectual Disabilities, 18,* 281–294.

Fotti, S. A., Katz, L. Y., Affi, T. O., & Cox, B. J. (2006). The associations between peer and parental relationships and suicidal behaviors in early adolescents. *Canadian Journal of Psychiatry, 51(11),* 698–703.

Fullan, M., Hill, P., & Crévola, C. (2006). *Breakthrough.* Thousand Oaks, CA: Corwin Press.

Geierstanger, S. P., Amaral, G., Mansour, M., & Walters, S. R. (2004). School-based health centers and academic performance: Research, challenges, and recommendations. *Journal of School Health, 4(9),* 347–352.

Goldman, J., Salus, M. K., Wolcott D., & Kennedy, K. Y. (2003). *A Coordinated Response to Child Abuse and Neglect: The Foundation for Practice.* Washington, DC: Government Printing Office.

Grogan-Kaylor, A., Ruffolo, M. C., Ortega, R. M., & Clarke, J. (2008). Behaviors of youth involved in the child welfare system. *Child Abuse & Neglect, 32(1),* 35–49.

Hagele, D. M. (2005). The impact of maltreatment on the developing child. *North Carolina Medical Journal, 66(5),* 356–359.

Hahn, R., Fuqua-Whitley, D., Wethington, H., Lowy, J, Liberman, A., Crosby, A., Fullilove, M., Johnson, R., Moscicki, E., Price, L., Snyder, S. R., Tuma, F., Cory, S., Stone, G., Mukhopadhaya, K., Chattopadhyay, S., & Dahlberg, L. (2007). The effectiveness of universal school-based programs for the prevention of violent and aggressive behavior: A report on recommendations of the task force on community preventive services. *Morbidity & Mortality Weekly Report, 55, RR-7,* 1–11.

Hale, J. B., Hoeppner, J. B., DeWitt, M. B., Coury, D. L., Ritacco, D. G., & Trommer, B. (1998). Evaluating medication response in ADHD: Cognitive, behavioral, and single-subject methodology. *Journal of Learning Disabilities, 31(6),* 595–607.

Hallahan, D. P., Keller, C. E., Martinez, E .A., Byrd, E. S., Gelman, J. A., & Xi-tao, F. (2007). How variable are interstate prevalence rates of learning disabilities and other special education categories? A longitudinal comparison. *Exceptional Children, 73(2),* 136–146.

Hargreaves, A., & Shirley, D. (2009). *The Fourth Way: The Inspiring Future for Educational Change.* Thousand Oaks, CA: Corwin Press.

Havey, J. M., Olson, J. M., & McCormick, C. (2005). Teachers' perceptions of the incidence and management of attention-deficit hyperactivity disorder. *Applied Neuropsychology, 12(2),* 120–127.

Heathfield, L. T., & Clark, E. (2004). Shifting from categories to services: Comprehensive school-based mental health for children with emotional disturbance and social maladjustment. *Psychology in the Schools, 41(8),* 911–920.

Hener, G. R., Knightly, C. A., & Steinberg, A. G. (2002). Hearing: Sounds and silences. In M. L. Batshaw (Ed.), *Children with Disabilities* (pp. 389–416). Baltimore, MD: Paul H. Brooks Publishing Co.

Henry, K. L. (2007). Who's skipping school: Characteristics of truants in 8th and 10th grade. *Journal of School Health, 77(1),* 29–35.

Herba, C. M., Ferdinand, R. F., van der Ende, J., Verhulst, F. C. (2007). Long term association of childhood suicide ideation. *Journal of the American Academy of Child and Adolescent Psychiatry, 46(11),* 1473–1481.

Hewitt, M., Weiner, S. L., & Simone, J. V. (2003). *Childhood Cancer Survivorship: Improving Care and Quality of Life.* Washington, DC: National Academies Press.

Hoagwood, K. E., Oline, S. S., Kerker, B. D., Kratochwill, T. R., Crowe, M., & Saka, N. (2007). Empirically based school interventions targeted at academic and mental health functioning. *Journal of Emotional and Behavioral Disorders, 15(2),* 66–92.

Hoffmann, J.P. (2006). Family structure, community context, and adolescent problem behaviors. *Journal of Youth and Adolescence, 35(6),* 867–880.

Hussey, J. M., Chang, J. J., & Kotch, J. B. (2006). Child maltreatment in the United States: Prevalence, risk factors, and adolescent health consequences. *Pediatrics, 118 (3),* 933–942.

Isaacs, D. (2006). Attention-deficit/hyperactivity disorder: Are we medicating for social disadvantage? *Journal of Paediatrics and Child Health, 42,* 544–547.

Jenkins, J., Simpson, A., Dunn, J., Rasbash, J., & O'Connor, T. G. (2005). Mutual influence of marital conflict and children's behavior problems: Shared and non-shared family risks. *Child Development, 76(1),* 25–39.

Jennings, J., Pearson, G., & Harris, M. (2000). Implementing and maintaining school-based mental health services in a large, urban school district. *Journal of School Health, 70(5),* 201–205.

Jerrom, C. (2003). Young offenders report a high level of depression and a lack of support. *Community Care, 1483.*

Jonson-Reid, M., Jiyoung, K., Barolak, M., Citerman, B., Laudel, C., Essma, A., Fezzi, N., Green, D., Kontak, D., Mueller, N., & Thomas, C. (2007). Maltreated children in the schools: The interface of school social work and child welfare. *Children & Schools, 29(3),* 182–191.

Jozefowicz-Simbeni, D. M. H. (2008). An ecological and developmental perspective on dropout risk factors in early adolescence: Role of school social workers in dropout prevention efforts. *Children and Schools, 30(1),* 49–62.

Kearney, C. A. (2007). Forms and functions of school refusal behavior in youth: An empirical analysis of absenteeism severity. *Journal of Child Psychology and Psychiatry, 48(1),* 53–61.

———. (2008). School absenteeism and school refusal behavior in youth: A contemporary review. *Clinical Psychology Review, 28(3),* 451–471.

Kilpatrick, D. G., Ruggiero, K. J., Acierno, R., Saunders, B. E., Resnick, H. S., & Best, C. L. (2003). Violence and risk of PTSD, major depression, substance abuse/dependence, and comorbidity: Results from the National Survey of Adolescents. *Journal of Consulting and Clinical Psychology, 71(4),* 692–700.

Kinzie, J. D. (2006). Traumatized refugee children: The case for individualized diagnosis and treatment. *Journal of Nervous and Mental Diseases, 194(7),* 534–537.

Kirby, M. J. L., & Keon, W. J. (2006). *Out of the Shadows at Last: Transforming Mental Health, Mental Illness and Addiction Services in Canada.* Ottawa: Senate of Canada Standing Senate Committee on Social Affairs, Science and Technology.

Koller, J. R., & Bertel, J. M. (2006). Responding to today's mental health needs of children, families and schools: Revisiting the preservice training and preparation of school-based personnel. *Education and Treatment of Children, 29(2),* 197–217.

Kowalski, R. M., & Limber, S. P. (2007). Electronic bullying among middle school students. *Journal of Adolescent Health, 41(6),* 522–530.

Kumpulainen, K. (2002). Phenomenology and treatment of selective mutism. *CNS Drugs, 16(3),* 175–180.

Kutash, K., Duchnowski, A. J., & Lynn, N. (2006). *School-based Mental Health: An Empirical Guide for Decision Makers.* Tampa, FL: The Research and Training Center for Children's Mental Health, Louis de la Parte Florida Mental Health Institute, University of South Florida.

Langley, A. K., Bergman, R. L., & Piacentini, J. C. (2002). Assessment of childhood anxiety. *International Journal of Psychiatry, 14,* 102–113.

Learning Disabilities Association of Ontario. Definition of learning disabilities. Retrieved January 10, 2008, from www.ldao.ca/what_are_lds/WorkingDescription.php.

Lerner, J. W., & Johns, Beverly. (2008). *Learning Disabilities and Related Mild Disabilities.* Boston: Houghton Mifflin Harcourt.

Lever, N. A., & Weist, M. D. (2006). School mental health and system transformation in Maryland. Presented at Mental Hygiene Administration's Annual Conference Transforming Mental Health Together, Baltimore, MD, May 2006.

Levine, M. (2001). *Educational Care: A System for Understanding and Helping Children with Learning Differences at Home and at School* (2nd ed.). Cambridge, MA: Educators Publishing Service.

Lindsay, G. (2007). Annual review: Educational psychology and the effectiveness of inclusive education/mainstreaming. *British Journal of Educational Psychology, 77(1),* 1–24.

Literacy and Numeracy Secretariat, Ontario Ministry of Education. (2006). *Making It Happen: The Report from the Literacy and Numeracy Secretariat.* Toronto: Author.

Lynn, C. J., McKay, M. M., & Atkins, M. S. (2003). School social work: Meeting the mental health needs of students through collaborations with teachers. *Children and Schools, 25(4),* 197–209.

MacMillan, K. M., & Violato, C. (2008). Pathways to competence: Parental adversity and the roles of parenting quality and social support. *Journal of Psychology, 142(4),* 427–444.

March, J. S., & Mulle, K. (1998). *OCD in Children and Adolescents: A Cognitive-Behavioral Treatment Manual.* New York: Guilford Press.

Margai, F., & Henry, N. (2003). A community-based assessment of learning disabilities using environmental and contextual risk factors. *Social Science and Medicine, 56 (5),* 1073–1086.

Marsee, M. A. (2008). Reactive aggression and posttraumatic stress in adolescents affected by Hurricane Katrina. *Journal of Clinical Child & Adolescent Psychology, 37(3),* 519–529.

Martinez, R. S., & Nellis, L. M. (2008). Response to intervention: A school-wide approach for promoting academic wellness for all students. In B. Doll & J.A. Cummings (Eds.), *Transforming School Mental Health Services: Population-based Approaches to Promoting the Competency and Wellness of Children* (pp 143–164). Thousand Oaks, CA: Corwin Press.

Martinussen, R., & Tannock, R. (2006). Working memory impairments in children with attention-deficit hyperactivity disorder with and without comorbid language learning disorders. *Journal of Clinical and Experimental Neuropsychology, 28(7),* 1073–1094.

Masia-Warner, C., Nangle, D.W., & Hansen, D.J. (2006). Bringing evidence-based child mental health services to schools: General issues and specific populations. *Education and Treatment of Children, 29(2),* 165–172.

Massey, O.T., Armstrong, K., Boroughs, M., Henson, K., & McCash, L. (2005). Mental health services in schools: A qualitative analysis of challenges to implementation, operation and sustainability. *Psychology in the Schools, 42(4),* 361–372.

Mazza, J. J., & Reynolds, W. M. (2008). School-side approaches to prevention of and intervention for depression and suicidal behaviors. In B. Doll & J.A. Cummings (Eds.), *Transforming School Mental Health Services: Population-based Approaches to Promoting the Competency and Wellness of Children* (pp 213–241). Thousand Oaks, CA: Corwin Press.

McCook, J. E. (2006). *The RTI Guide: Developing and Implementing a Model in Your Schools.* Horsham, PA: LRP Publications.

McLoone, J., Hudson, J. L., & Rapee, R. M. (2006). Treating anxiety disorders in a school setting. *Education and Treatment of Children, 20(2),* 219–242.

McMurtry, R., & Curling, A. (2008). *The Roots of Youth Violence*. Toronto: Queen's Printer for Ontario.

Merrell, K. W., Gueldner, B. A., & Tran, O. K. (2008). Social and emotional learning. In B. Doll & J. A. Cummings (Eds.), *Transforming School Mental Health Services: Population-based Approaches to Promoting the Competency and Wellness of Children* (pp. 165–185). Thousand Oaks, CA: Corwin Press.

Mills, C., Hoover Stephan, S., Moore, E., Weist, M. D., Daly, B. P., & Edwards, M. (2006). The President's New Freedom Commission: Capitalizing on opportunities to advance school-based mental health services. *Clinical Child and Family Psychology Review, 9(3)*, 149–161.

Mishna, F., Pepler, D., & Weiner, J. (2006). Factors associated with perceptions and responses to bullying situations by children, parents, teachers and principals. *Victims and Offenders, 1*, 255–288.

Mureika, J. M. K., Falconer, R. D., & Howard, B. M. (2004). The changing role of the school psychologist: From tester to collaborator. *Canadian Association of School Psychologists and Psychologists in Education Newsletter*, 6–8.

Nabors, L. A., & Lehmkuhl, H. D. (2004). Children with chronic medical conditions: Recommendations for school mental health clinicians. *Journal of Developmental and Physical Disabilities, 16(1)*, 1–15.

Nabors, L. A., & Reynolds, M. W. (2000). Program evaluation activities: Outcomes related to treatment for adolescents receiving school-based mental health services. *Children's Services: Social Policy, Research and Practice, 3(3)*, 175–189.

Nabors, L. A., Weist, M. D., & Reynolds, M. W. (2000). Overcoming challenges in outcome evaluations of school mental health programs. *Journal of School Health, 70(5)*, 206–209.

Neild, R. C., Balfranz, R., & Herzog, L. (2007). An early warning system. *Educational Leadership*, October, 28–33.

Neild, R. C., Stoner-Eby, S., & Furstenberg, F. (2008). Connecting entrance and departure: The transition to ninth grade and high school. *Education & Urban Society, 40(5)*, 543–569.

Neuman, S. B. (2008). Get bolder in effort to lift all children's education. *Detroit Free Press*, July 31, 2008.

Nicholas, J. S., Charles, J. M., Carpenter, L. A., King, L. B., Jenner, W., & Spratt, E. G. (2008). Prevalence and characteristics of children with autism spectrum disorders. *Annals of Epidemiology, 182*, 130–136.

Nielson, M. E. (2002). Gifted students with learning disabilities: Recommendations for identification and programming. *Exceptionality, 10(2)*, 93–111.

Nock, M. K., Kazdin, A. E., Hiripi, E., & Kessler, R. C. (2007). Lifetime prevalence, correlates and persistence of oppositional defiant disorder: Results from the National Comorbidity Survey Replication. *Journal of Child Psychology and Psychiatry, 48(7)*, 703–713.

Nordness, P. D. (2005). A comparison of school-based and community-based adherence during wraparound family planning meetings. *Education and Treatment of Children, 28(3)*, 308–320.

O'Connell, R. G., Bellgrove, M. A., Dockree, P. M., & Roberston, I. H. (2006). Cognitive remediation in ADHD: Effects of periodic noncontingent alerts on sustained attention to response. *Neuropsychological Rehabilitation, 16(6)*, 653–665.

Olweus, D. (1993). *Bullying at School: What We Know and What We Can Do.* Cambridge, MA: Blackwell.

Onyskiw, J. E. (2007). The link between family violence and cruelty to family pets. *Journal of Emotional Abuse, 7(3)*, 7–30.

Ontario Ministry of Children and Youth Services. (2006). *A Shared Responsibility: Ontario's Policy Framework for Child and Youth Mental Health.* Toronto: Author.

———. (2008). *Realizing Potential: Our Children, Our Youth, Our Future, Ontario Ministry of Children and Youth Services Strategic Framework 2008–2012.* Toronto: Author.

Ontario Ministry of Education. (2001). *Special Education: A Guide for Educators.* Toronto: Author.

———. (2003a). *Building Pathways to Success: The Report of the Program Pathways for Students at Risk Work Group, Grades 7–12.* Toronto: Author.

———. (2003b). *Think Literacy Success: The Report of the Expert Panel on Students at Risk in Ontario, Grades 7–12.* Toronto: Author.

———. (2005). *Education for All: The Report of the Expert Panel on Literacy and Numeracy Instruction for Students with Special Education Needs, Kindergarten to Grade 6,* Toronto: Author.

———. (2006). *Special Education Transformation: The Report of the Co-chairs with the Recommendations of the Working Table on Special Education.* Toronto: Author.

———. (2008a). *Finding Common Ground: Character Development in Ontario Schools, K–12.* Toronto: Author.

———. (2008b). *Reach Every Student: Energizing Ontario Education.* Toronto: Author.

Paternité, C. (2005). School-based mental health programs and services: Overview and introduction to the special issue. *Journal of Abnormal Child Psychology, 6*, 657–663.

Paternité, C. E., & Johnston, T. C. (2005). Rational and strategies for central involvement of educators in effective school-based mental health programs. *Journal of Youth and Adolescence, 34*, 41–49.

Paternité, C. E., Shilling, K., Graff-Reed, R., & McLaughlin, M. (2008). "Alternative education" and "Alternative school discipline" programs in Butler County (OH)—Narrative summary of Phase 1 formative evaluation. Retrieved February 6, 2008, from www.units.muohio.edu/csbmbp/resources/alted/alted-phase1summ.pdf.

Pelkonen, M., & Marttnunen, M. (2003). Child and adolescent suicide: Epidemiology, risk factors and approaches to prevention. *Pediatric Drugs, 5(4)*, 243–255.

Pepler, D. J., Craig, W. M., Connolly, J. A., Yiule, A., McMaster, L., & Jiang, D. (2006). A developmental perspective on bullying. *Aggressive Behavior, 32,* 376–384.

Phelps, L., Brown, R. T., & Power, T. J. (2002). *Pediatric Psychopharmacology: Combining Medical and Psychosocial Interventions.* Washington, DC: American Psychological Association.

Pincus, D. B., & Friedman, A. G. (2004). Improving children's coping with everyday stress: Transporting treatment interventions to the school setting. *Clinical Child and Family Psychology Review, 7(4),* 223–240.

President's New Freedom Commission on Mental Health. (2003). *Achieving the Promise: Transforming Mental Health Care in America. Final Report for the President's New Freedom Commission on Mental Health (SMA Publication No. 03–3832).* Rockville, MD: Author.

Pumariega, A. J., & Vance, H. R. (1999). School-based mental health services: The foundation of systems of care for children's mental health. *Psychology in the Schools, 36(5),* 371–378.

Quinn, M. M., & Poirier, J. M. (2006). *Study of Effective Alternative Education Programs: Final Grant Report.* Washington, DC: American Institutes for Research.

Quinn, M. M., Rutherford, R. B., & Leone, P. B. (2001). Students with disabilities in correctional facilities. *ERIC Digest, ED461598, 2001–12–00,* 1–6.

Reber, M. (2002). Dual diagnosis: Mental retardation psychiatric disorders. In M.L. Batshaw (Ed.), *Children with Disabilities* (pp. 389–416). Baltimore, MD: Paul H. Brooks Publishing Co.

Reddy, L. A., & Richardson, L. (2006). School-based prevention and intervention programs for children with emotional disturbance. *Education and Treatment of Children, 29(2),* 379–404.

Repie, M. S. (2005). A school mental health issues survey from the perspective of regular and special education teachers, school counselors and school psychologists. *Education and Treatment of Children, 28(3),* 279–298.

Rideout, V. (2007). *Parents, Children & Media.* Menlo Park, CA: Henry J. Kaiser Family Foundation.

Riehl, C. (2000). The principal's role in creating inclusive schools for diverse students: A review of normative, empirical, and critical literature on the practice of educational administration. *Review of Educational Research, 70,* 55–81.

Ringeisen, H., Henderson, K., & Hoagwood, K. (2003). Context matters: Schools and the "research to practice gap" in children's mental health. *School Psychology Review, 32(2),* 153–168.

Roberts, A. (2006). Classification typology and assessment of five levels of woman battering. *Journal of Family Violence, 21(8),* 521–527.

Roberts, D. F., Foehr, U. G., & Rideout, V. (2005). *Generation M: Media in the Lives of 8–18 Year Olds.* Menlo Park, CA: The Henry J. Kaiser Family Foundation.

Roberts, R. E., Roberts, C. R., & Xing, Y. (2007). Rates of DSM-IV psychiatric disorders among adolescents in a large metropolitan area. *Journal of Psychiatric Research, 41(11),* 959–967.

Robertson, H-J. (2006). Dropouts or leftouts? School leavers in Canada. *Phi Delta Kappan, 87(9)*, 715–717.

Rones, M., & Hoagwood, K. (2000). School-based mental health services: A research review. *Clinical Child and Family Psychology Review, 3*, 223–241.

Rosenberg, H. J., Jankowski, M. K., Sengupta, A., Wolfe, R.S., Wolford, G.L., & Rosenberg, S.D. (2006). Suicide and multiple suicide attempts and associated health risk factors in New Hampshire adolescents. *Suicide and Life-threatening Behavior, 35(5)*, 63–73.

Rowland, A. S., Umbach, D. M., Catoe, K. E., Stallone, L., Long, S., Rabiner, D., Naftel, A. J., Panke, D., Faulk, R., & Sandler D. P. (2001). Studying the epidemiology of attention-deficit hyperactivity disorder: screening method and pilot results. *Canadian Journal of Psychiatry, 46(10)*, 931–940.

Rowling, L. (2007). School mental health: Politics, power and practice. *Advances in School Mental Health, 1(1)*, 23–31.

Sacks, S. Z., Wolffe, K. E., & Tierney, D. (1998). Lifestyles of students with visual impairments: Preliminary studies of social networks. *Exceptional Children, 64*, 463–478.

Saklofske, D. H., Schwean, V. L., Bartell, R., Mureika, J. M. K., Andrews, J., Derevensky, J., & Janzen, H. L. (2007). School psychology in Canada: Past, present, and future perspectives. In T. Fagan & P. Wise (Eds.), *School Psychology: Past, Present, and Future Perspectives* (pp. 297–337). Bethesda, MD: National Association of School Psychologists.

Sandomierski, T., Kincaid, D., & Algozzine, B. (2008). Response to intervention and positive behavior support: Brothers from different mothers or sisters with different misters? Retrieved August 22, 2008, from pbis.org/news/New/Newsletters/Newsletter4–2.aspx.

Santiago, E., Ferrara, J., & Blank, M. (2008). A full-service school fulfills its promise. *Educational Leadership, 65(7)*, 44–47.

School-Based Adolescent Health Care Program. (1993). *The Answer Is at School: Bringing Health Care to Our Students*. Washington, DC: Robert Wood Johnson Foundation.

Seigel, J. A., & Cole, E. (2003). Role expansion for school psychologists: Challenges and future directions. In E. Cole & J. Siegel (Eds.), *Effective Consultation in School Psychology* (pp. 3–23). Cambridge, MA: Hogrefe & Huber.

Shaw, S. (1999). The devolution of interest in slow learners: Can we continue to ignore? *NASP Communiqué, 31*.

Short, R. J., & Stein, W. (2008). Behavioral and social epidemiology: Population-based problem identification and monitoring. In B. Doll & J.A. Cummings (Eds.), *Transforming School Mental Health Services: Population-based Approaches to Promoting the Competency and Wellness of Children* (pp. 23–42). Thousand Oaks, CA: Corwin Press.

Singer, H. (2005). Tourette's syndrome: From behavior to biology. *Lancet Neurology, 4(3)*, 149–159.

Slade, E. P. (2003). The relationship between school characteristics and the availability of mental health and related health services in middle and high schools in the United States. *Journal of Behavioral Health Services and Research, 30(4),* 382–392.

Smith, P. K., Mahdavi, J., Carvalho, M., Fisher, S., Russell, S., & Tippett, N. (2008). Cyberbullying: Its nature and impact in secondary school pupils. *Journal of Child Psychology and Psychiatry, and Allied Disciplines, 49(4),* 376–385.

Smith, T. J., & Adams, G. (2006). The effect of comorbid AD/HD and learning disabilities on parent-reported behavioral and academic outcomes in children. *Learning Disability Quarterly, 29,* 101–112.

Snowling, M. J., Bishop, D. V. M., Stothard, S. E., Chipchase, B., & Kaplan, C. (2006). Psychosocial outcomes at 15 years of children with a preschool history of speech-language impairment. *Journal of Child Psychology and Psychiatry, 47(8),* 759–765.

Spilsbury, J. C., Kahana, S., Drotar, D., Creeden, R., Flannery, D. J., & Friedman, S. (2008). Profiles of behavioral problems in children who witness domestic violence. *Violence and Victims, 23(1),* 3–17.

Steele, M. M., & Doey, T. (2007). Suicidal behavior in children and adolescents. Part 2: Treatment and prevention. *Canadian Journal of Psychiatry, 52(6), Supplement 1,* 35S–45S.

Stein, M. A., Efron, L. A., Schiff, W. B., & Glanzman, M. (2002). Attention deficits and hyperactivity. In M. L. Batshaw (Ed.), *Children with Disabilities* (pp. 389–416). Baltimore, MD: Paul H. Brooks Publishing Co.

Stuart, S. (2002). Communication: Speech and Language. In M. L. Batshaw (Ed.), *Children with Disabilities* (pp. 389–416). Baltimore, MD: Paul H. Brooks Publishing Co.

Swearer, S. M., Espelage, D. L., Love, K. B. & Kingsbury, W. (2008). School-wide approaches to intervention for school aggression and bullying. In B. Doll & J.A. Cummings (Eds.), *Transforming School Mental Health Services: Population-based Approaches to Promoting the Competency and Wellness of Children* (pp 187–212). Thousand Oaks, CA: Corwin Press.

Tannock, R., & Martinussen, R. (2001). Reconceptualizing ADHD. *Educational Leadership, 59(3),* 20–25.

Taubin, K. E., Mauk, J. E., & Batshaw, M. L. (2002). Pervasive developmental disorders. In M. L. Batshaw (Ed.), *Children with Disabilities* (pp. 389–416). Baltimore, MD: Paul H. Brooks Publishing Co.

Teich, J. L., Robinson, G., & Weist, M. D. (2007). What kinds of mental health services do public schools in the United States provide? *Advances in School Mental Health, 1(1),* 13–22

Trocmé, N., Fallon, B., MacLaurin, B., Daciuk, J., Felstiner, C., & Black, T. (2005). Canadian incidence study of reported child abuse and neglect, CIS-2003. Major Findings Report. Ottawa: Public Health Agency of Canada

Trocmé, N., Tourigny, M., MacLaurin, B., & Fallon, B. (2003). Major findings from the Canadian incidence study of reported child abuse and neglect. *Child Abuse & Neglect, 27(12)*, 1427.

Tyler, S., Allison, K., & Winsler. (2006). Child neglect: Developmental consequences, intervention and policy implications. *Child & Youth Care Forum, 35(1)*, 1–20.

UNICEF. (2007). *Child Poverty in Perspective: An Overview of Child Well-Being in Rich Countries. Innocenti Report Card 7*. Florence, Italy: Author.

U.S. Department of Education. Office of Elementary and Secondary Education. (2002). *No Child Left Behind: A Desktop Reference*. Washington, DC: Author.

U.S. Department of Health and Human Services (DHHS). (1999). *Mental Health: A Report of the Surgeon General*. Rockville, MD: U.S. Department of Health and Human Services, Substance Abuse and Mental Health Services Administration, Center for Mental Health Services, National Institutes of Health, National Institute of Mental Health.

Vanderbleek, L. M. (2004). Engaging families in school-based mental health treatment. *Journal of Mental Health Counselling. 26(3)*, 211–224.

Waddell, C. Hua, J. M., Garland, O. M., Peters, R. D., & McEwan, K. (2007). Preventing mental disorders in children. *Canadian Journal of Public Health, 98(3)*, 166–173.

Waddell, C., McEwan, K., Shepherd, C. A., Offord, D. R. (2005). A public health strategy to improve the mental health of Canadian children. *Canadian Journal of Psychiatry*, 58(4), 226–233.

Wadsworth, M. E., Raviv, T., & Reinhard, C. (2008). An indirect effects model of the association between poverty and child functioning: The role of children's poverty-related stress. *Journal of Loss and Trauma, 13(2–3)*, 156–185.

Wagner, M., Kutash, K., Duchnowski, A. J., Epstein, M. H., & Sumi, W. C. (2005). A national picture of the characteristics of students with emotional disturbances receiving special education. *Journal of Emotional and Behavioral Disorders, 13(2)*, 79–96.

Waldrop, A. E., Hansen, R.F., Resnick, H. S., Kilpatrick, D. G., Naugle, A. E., & Saunders, B. E. (2007). Risk factors for suicidal behavior among a national sample of adolescents: Implications for prevention. *Journal of Traumatic Stress, 20(5)*, 869–879.

Wall, R., & Corn, A. L. (2004). Students with visual impairments in Texas: Description and extrapolation of data. *Journal of Visual Impairment and Blindness, 98(6)*, 341–350.

Wazana, A., Bresnahan, M., & Kline, J. (2007). The Autism epidemic: Fact or artifact? *Journal of the American Academy of Child and Adolescent Psychiatry, 46(6)*, 721–730.

Weist, M. D. (2005). Fulfilling the promise of school-based mental health: Moving toward a public mental health promotion approach. *Journal of Abnormal Child Psychology, 33(6)*, 735–741.

Weist, M. D., Ambrose, M. G., & Lewis, C. (2006). Expanded school mental health: A collaborative community-school example. *Children & Schools, 28(1)*, 45–50.

Weist, M. D., & Paternité, C. E. (2006). Building an interconnected policy-training practice-research agenda to advance school mental health. *Education and Treatment of Children, 29(2)*, 173–196.

Weist, M. D., Rubin, M., Moore, E., Adelsheim, S., & Wrobel, G. (2007), Mental health screening in schools. *Journal of School Health, 77(2)*, 53–58.

Weist, M. D., Sander, M. A., Walrath, C., Link, B., Nabors, L., Adelsheim, S., Moore, E., Jennings, J., & Carrillo, K. (2005). Developing principals for best practice in expanded school mental health. *Journal of Youth and Adolescence, 34(1)*, 7–13.

Wolff, J. C., & Ollendick, T. H. (2006). The comorbidity of conduct problems and depression in childhood and adolescence. *Clinical Child and Family Psychology Review, 9 (3/4)*, 201–220.

Wunsch, M. J., Conlon, C. J., & Scheidt, P. C. (2002). Substance abuse: A preventable threat to development. In M. L. Batshaw (Ed.), *Children with Disabilities* (pp. 389–416). Baltimore, MD: Paul H. Brooks Publishing Co.

Zins, J. E., Bloodworth, M. R., Weissberg, R. P., & Walberg, H. J. (2004). The scientific base linking social and emotional learning to school success. In J. E. Zins, R. P. Weissberg, M. C. Wang, & H. J. Walberg (Eds.), *Building Academic Success on Social Emotional Learning: What Does the Research Say?* (pp. 3–22). New York: Teachers College Press.

ABOUT THE AUTHORS

Debra S. Lean, PhD, CPsych, has more than twenty years of experience in children's mental health and school psychology. She was a staff psychologist and led the Learning Disability Clinic at a psychiatric hospital-based child and family mental health clinic. Dr. Lean has worked as a school psychologist for thirteen years where she provided assessment and therapy services to elementary and high school students. She has been the chief psychologist at the Dufferin-Peel Catholic District School Board, Ontario, Canada, for eight years and also consults to the board's primary level Autism Spectrum Disorder class. Dr. Lean has initiated numerous innovative programs in the Psychology Department, including specialty services in the autism, neuropsychology, and mental health areas. She is a member of several committees at the Provincial Centre of Excellence for Children and Youth Mental Health at The Children's Hospital of Eastern Ontario. She has made many presentations to teachers, parents, and mental health professionals. Dr. Lean has a particular interest in broadening the role of professional student services personnel, especially in prevention and early identification of mental health problems in students.

Vincent A. Colucci, MSW, RSW, has more than thirty years of professional social work experience in the fields of mental health and education. He has worked in a hospital and a community agency setting providing individual, group, and family therapy. His current responsibilities at the Dufferin-Peel Catholic District School Board include working with students in regular, special, and alternative programs in the elementary and high school levels. Mr. Colucci is a proponent of school-based support services and of a population-based approach to servicing students. He counsels students and parents, consults to school personnel, and has been a member of numerous

119

school board committees. He has been a field supervisor of social work students, board member of a community agency, and vice president of the Alternative Education Association. Mr. Colucci is a trained restorative justice facilitator. He has made presentations to professional colleagues both in Canada and in the United States.

Breinigsville, PA USA
08 September 2010
245002BV00001B/5/P